BRAIN SCIENCE

▲ by Melissa Abramovitz

Content Consultant

Augusto Miravalle, MD
Associate Professor of Neurology
University of Colorado Denver School of Medicine

Essential Library
An Imprint of Abdo Publishing | abdopublishing.com

CUTTING EDGE
SCIENCE + TECHNOLOGY

abdopublishing.com

Published by Abdo Publishing, a division of ABDO, PO Box 398166, Minneapolis, Minnesota 55439. Copyright © 2016 by Abdo Consulting Group, Inc. International copyrights reserved in all countries. No part of this book may be reproduced in any form without written permission from the publisher. Essential Library™ is a trademark and logo of Abdo Publishing.

Printed in the United States of America, North Mankato, Minnesota
092015
012016

THIS BOOK CONTAINS
RECYCLED MATERIALS

Cover Photo: Pasieka/Science Source

Interior Photos: Shutterstock Images, 4–5; Paulo Whitaker/Reuters/Newscom, 7; iStockphoto, 8, 16, 21, 47, 53; Amelie-Benoist/BSIP/Corbis, 11; Oli Scarff/Getty Images, 14; Henry Rivers/iStockphoto, 17; Tom Barrick/Chris Clark/SGHMS/Science Source, 18–19; Simon Fraser/Science Source, 23; Heiti Paves/Science Source, 24; Anthony Zador, 27; Riccardo Cassiani-Ingoni/Science Source, 28–29; John B. Carnett/Popular Science/Getty Images, 31; Deposit Photos/Glow Images, 33; Science Source, 34, 58–59; D. Silbersweig/Science Source, 38–39; Gary Carlson/Science Source, 41; Centers for Disease Control and Prevention, 44; David Mack/Science Source, 48–49; Voisin/Phanie Sarl/Corbis, 51; Ted S. Warren/AP Images, 55; David Walter Banks/For The Washington Post/Getty Images, 57; NAP/AP Images, 60; Carol & Mike Werner/Visuals Unlimited/Corbis, 63; Biophoto Associates/Science Source, 65; Philippe Psaila/Science Source, 68–69; Sean Gallup/Getty Images, 72; Brian Kersey/AP Images, 75; John Gress/Corbis, 77; Henning Dalhoff/Science Source, 78–79; Aly Song/Reuters/Corbis, 81; University of Southern California, 83; Kenneth K. Lam/Baltimore Sun/MCT/Newscom, 84; Charles Dharapak/AP Images, 88–89; Defense Advanced Research Projects Agency, 91; Itsuo Inouye/AP Images, 93; Sang Tan/AP Images, 96; F. Astier/Centre Hospitalier Régional Universitaire de Lille/Science Source, 98

Editor: Arnold Ringstad
Series Designer: Craig Hinton

Library of Congress Control Number: 2015945642

Cataloging-in-Publication Data
Abramovitz, Melissa.
  Brain science / Melissa Abramovitz.
   p. cm. -- (Cutting-edge science and technology)
ISBN 978-1-62403-914-0 (lib. bdg.)
Includes bibliographical references and index.
1. Brain--Juvenile literature. 2. Central nervous system--Juvenile literature.
I. Title.
612.8/2--dc23

2015945642

CONTENTS

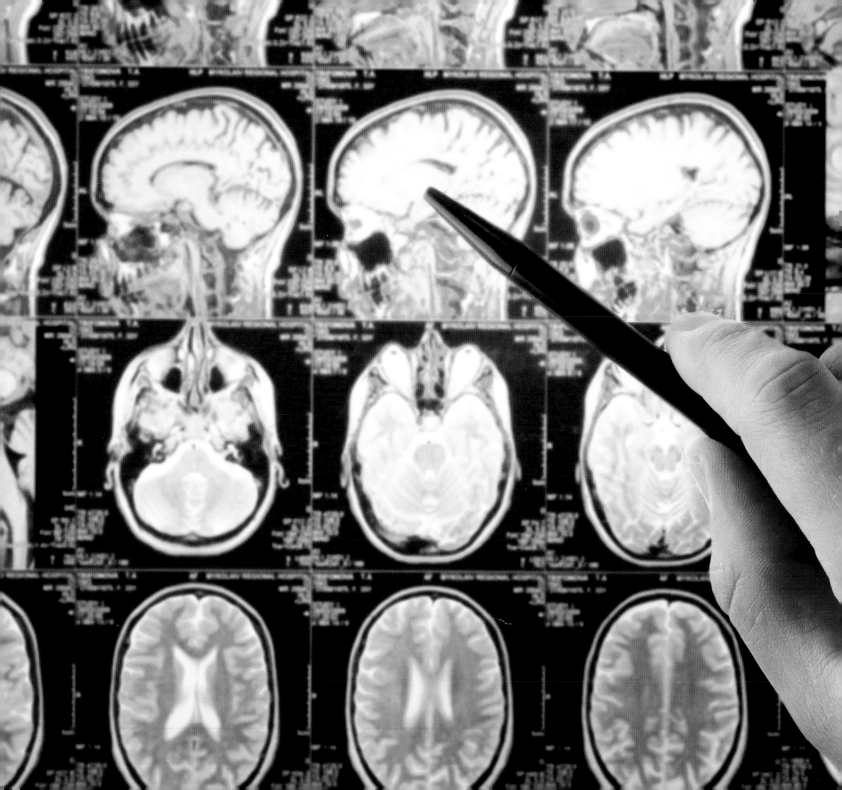

ONE

SENDING THOUGHTS FROM BRAIN TO BRAIN

In 2013, neuroscientists in North Carolina and Natal, Brazil, proved thoughts can be transmitted from one brain to another. This type of communication previously existed only in the realm of science fiction, where it is known as telepathy. In fact, when the scientists announced their findings, they compared the research to similar concepts from the Star Trek franchise of science fiction films and television shows. In Star Trek, the person transferring the thoughts simply touched the recipient's face. The real-life method is much more complex.

The neuroscientists used the Internet to transmit brain signals from a rat in Brazil to a rat in North Carolina. The second rat correctly interpreted the signals. Lead researcher Miguel Nicolelis of Duke University calls the phenomenon a brain-to-brain

Studying the brain has made it possible to build incredible brain-linked technology.

interface (BTBI). Earlier researchers created brain-to-machine interfaces that allowed people to use their thoughts to control computers. But this was the first time scientists had achieved a BTBI.

How They Did It

The Duke University researchers in North Carolina implanted electricity-conducting devices called electrodes into the brain of a rat they called a decoder rat. This rat was placed in an enclosure with two levers, one of which it could press to receive a sip of water. The decoder rat pushed the water lever 50 percent of the time, the expected result if the rat was randomly picking a lever.

Meanwhile, a second rat in Brazil, the encoder rat, sat in an identical enclosure. Researchers used light signals to train the encoder to press the water lever. The rat pressed the water lever correctly 95 percent of the time. Electrodes implanted in its brain recorded electric activity while the rat performed the task. The electric activity was converted into signals and sent to a computer to be transmitted over the Internet to the decoder rat's brain. When it received the signals, the decoder rat pressed the correct lever approximately 70 percent of the time.[1] The researchers got the same result when the encoder rat learned to identify the correct lever using touch rather than light signals.

◢ Telepathy and the Future

Miguel Nicolelis believes the two rats in his experiments worked cooperatively to achieve the lever tasks because each was rewarded only when the decoder rat chose the correct lever. He believes this principle could be expanded to include several brains cooperating to solve tasks no one person could solve alone. In addition, if methods of transmitting thoughts without the need to implant electrodes can be perfected, he believes this could allow people who do not speak the same language to communicate with their minds. People also could telepathically share their thoughts and emotions through the Internet, just like they share e-mails.

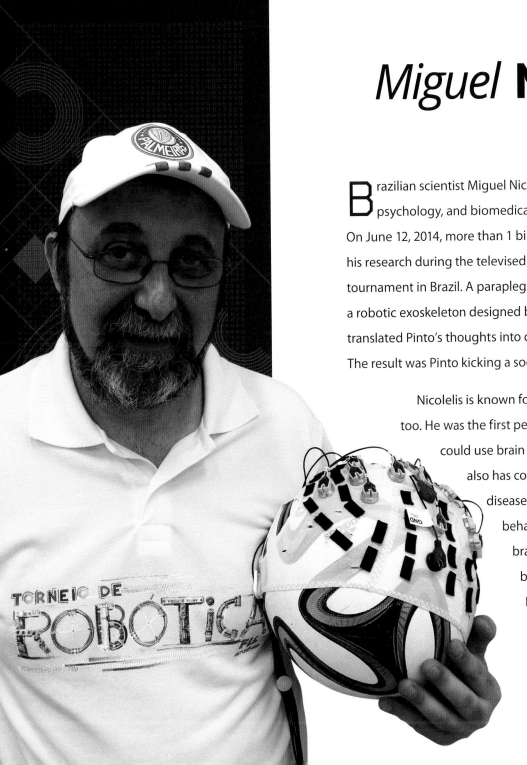

Miguel **Nicolelis**

(1961–)

Brazilian scientist Miguel Nicolelis is a professor of neurobiology, psychology, and biomedical engineering at Duke University. On June 12, 2014, more than 1 billion people witnessed the results of his research during the televised kickoff of the FIFA World Cup soccer tournament in Brazil. A paraplegic man named Juliano Pinto wore a robotic exoskeleton designed by Nicolelis. Computers in the suit translated Pinto's thoughts into commands that moved the exoskeleton. The result was Pinto kicking a soccer ball.

Nicolelis is known for other contributions to neuroscience, too. He was the first person to propose animals and people could use brain signals to control artificial limbs. Nicolelis also has contributed greatly to studying brain diseases by bringing together knowledge about behavior, cells, and brain systems. He believes brain diseases can be understood best by studying the molecules within cells. Problems at the molecular level can lead to abnormal cell activities, which can cause errors in brain circuits and give way to known symptoms and behaviors.

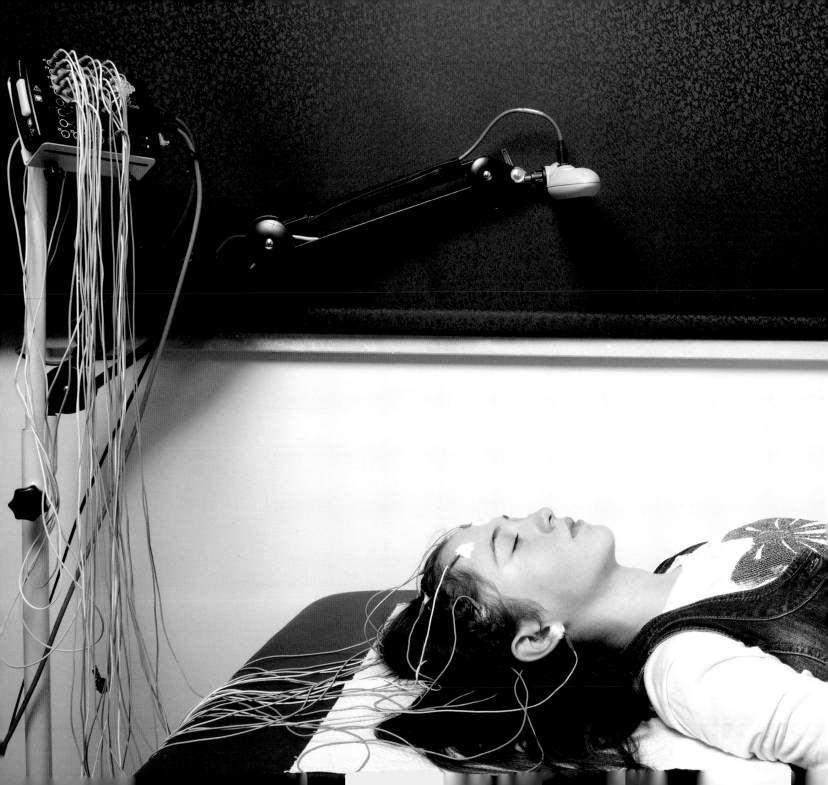

EEG machines are commonly used in brain research.

Human-to-Rat Telepathy

Soon after the Duke University study was published, other researchers provided further evidence a BTBI was possible. Scientists at Harvard University led by Seung-Schik Yoo tested a noninvasive BTBI. Unlike the Duke test, this team's research did not involve cutting into the head to place electrodes directly on the brain. Electrodes were placed on human volunteers' scalps and connected to an electroencephalograph (EEG) machine, a device that records electric activity in the brain. The rats in the study were hooked up to a focused ultrasound (FUS) machine. The machine focuses sound waves on a particular brain area. In this case, it was used to stimulate the part of the rats' brains that controls tail movement. A computer connected the EEG and FUS machines.

Researchers instructed each human volunteer to think about moving a rat's tail. The EEG recorded the brain signals created by this thought, and the computer sent the signals to a rat's brain through the FUS machine. The rats moved their tails 94 percent of the time.[2]

◄ Ethical Questions About Telepathy

Bioethicists, experts who study ethics in biological research, have raised questions about BTBIs. Bioethicists John Trimper, Paul Wolpe, and Karen Rommelfanger of Emory University believe reading or sending thoughts could be an invasion of personal privacy, especially if it is done without permission. They also worry that, since BTBIs can be transmitted over the Internet, hackers could interfere with people's neural devices. Other concerns include the ability for criminals to silently communicate crime plans and the possibility of emotional harm to test subjects. Bioethicists point out any technology can be used for good or bad. Still, technology writer Sebastian Anthony writes that BTBIs are "terrifying if you stop to think about the nefarious possibilities of a . . . dictatorship with mind control tech."[3]

⏴TMS Procedures

When a patient arrives for a TMS procedure to treat depression, migraines, or other issues, he or she first enters the treatment room and sits in a reclining chair. The patient puts on earplugs to protect against the loud noises of the TMS coil. The magnet is turned on, and its strength is increased until the patient's hands start twitching. This tells the doctor how intense the TMS should be. The procedure then begins. The patient feels clicking and tapping on his or her head. TMS typically lasts approximately 40 minutes.

Human-to-Human Telepathy

TMS involves generating a magnetic field in close proximity to the brain.

The work at Duke and Harvard showed animal-to-animal and human-to-animal brain communication is possible. In 2013, researchers at the University of Washington took the next step, creating a human-to-human brain interface. Computer science and engineering professor Rajesh Rao and psychology professor Andrea Stocco showed two human minds can communicate with thoughts. Rao wore a cap connected to an EEG machine, which was connected to a computer. Rao played a simple computer game using only his thoughts. Thoughts about actions create brain signals identical to those created when an action is actually performed.

In another building, Stocco wore a cap with a transcranial magnetic stimulation (TMS) coil placed over his left motor cortex, the area of the brain that controls movements of the right hand. TMS uses magnetic fields to influence specific areas of the brain. It has been used to treat migraines and depression, as well as to diagnose brain disorders. Stocco had a computer keyboard in front of him but no computer screen. He wore earphones that prevented him from hearing when the TMS coil became active.

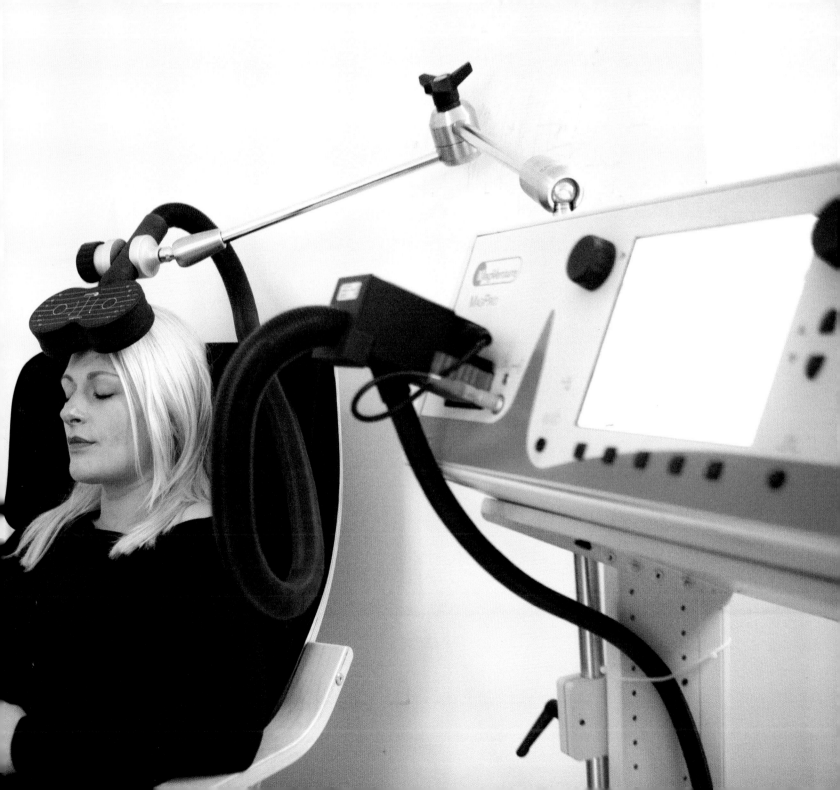

When Rao thought about moving his own hand to fire a cannon in the game, the computer transmitted his brain signals to activate the TMS coil. This process took less than a second. Stocco's right index finger involuntarily moved to push the key on the keyboard that would fire the cannon. Stocco said it felt like "a nervous tic."[4] Rao said, "It was both exciting and eerie to watch an imagined action from my brain get translated into actual action by another brain."[5]

Cutting-Edge Neuroscience

Through cutting-edge studies, scientists have made enormous progress in understanding what thoughts are and how the brain works. Still, scientists acknowledge the brain is the least-understood body system. Neuroscientist Christof Koch explains, "The human brain, with its eighty-six billion nerve cells, is the most complex piece of organized matter in the known universe."[6] To better understand this complicated organ, the US government initiated a multibillion dollar project called Brain Research Through Advancing Innovative Neurotechnologies

(BRAIN) in 2013. There are similar initiatives in Europe and Asia.

Everything the brain does, from thinking to feeling to controlling the body, depends on electric and chemical signals among its neurons, or nerve cells. One of the main goals of today's brain initiatives is to map the connections among neurons. Scientists estimate there are approximately 1 quadrillion neuron connections, so this is no small task.[7] Brain mapping involves matching neuron activity in particular areas of the brain to corresponding thoughts and behaviors. Neuroscientists, biologists, mathematicians, engineers, medical doctors, geneticists, computer scientists, and physicists are all participating in brain-mapping projects.

◢ How MRI Works

During an MRI scan, the patient lies in a large tube. Surrounding the patient is a large, powerful magnet. To attain this power, the magnet's components must be kept extremely cold using liquid helium. The magnet orients the atoms that make up the patient's body in one of two directions. About half are oriented in one direction, and about half are oriented in the other direction. However, a few atoms do not have counterparts. When the MRI machine sends radio waves into the body, these unmatched atoms switch directions. Then, when the radio waves stop, they switch back to their old orientation. This switch gives off energy. The MRI's scanning equipment detects this energy and uses it to build an image of the patient's body.

Making a Map

Scientists began mapping the brain into major areas, such as the cortex and limbic system, in the 1800s. The cortex governs thinking and reasoning, and the limbic system is important in emotion, memory, and motivation. Modern advances in computer science, genetics, and related technologies allow researchers to map the brain on a cellular level. Magnetic resonance imaging (MRI), which uses radio waves and magnets to construct three-dimensional images of the brain, and functional magnetic

resonance imaging (fMRI), which tracks brain activity in certain areas, are two key technologies that make this possible.

Neurologists are using advanced technologies to study other aspects of how human and animal brains store information, learn, and develop various illnesses. They hope this research will lead to effective treatments for brain disorders. For example, some scientists are studying the concept of cognitive reserve, the methods by which brains can adapt to physical damage without harming brain function. Other researchers are gaining insight into how genes and brain circuits cause disorders, such as depression. Some scientists are developing methods of erasing memories and implanting false memories in the brain. And others are creating technologies that allow people to control artificial limbs with their thoughts. As neuroscientist Anthony Zador wrote in 2014, "The rate of progress is staggering."[8]

BRAIN BASICS

B iologists divide the brain's structure into two halves, or hemispheres. Four main sections called lobes—the frontal, parietal, temporal, and occipital lobes—span both hemispheres. Different areas of the cortex, or outer section, of these lobes govern thinking and reasoning and process sensory information and language. Under the lobes is the limbic system, which plays a role in emotions and memory. The cerebellum, which regulates movement, also is under the lobes.

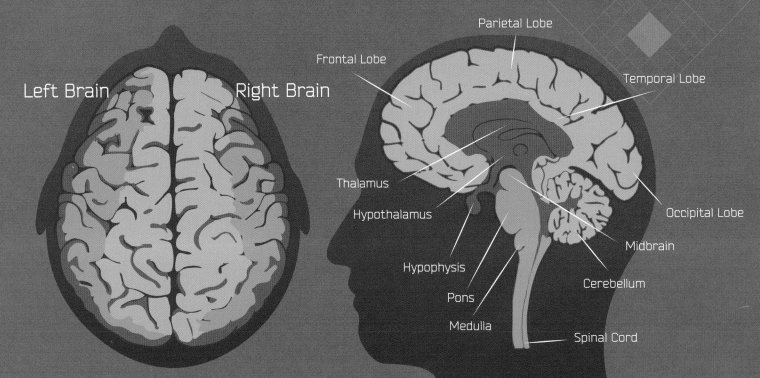

Left Brain
Right Brain

Parietal Lobe
Frontal Lobe
Temporal Lobe
Thalamus
Hypothalamus
Occipital Lobe
Midbrain
Hypophysis
Cerebellum
Pons
Medulla
Spinal Cord

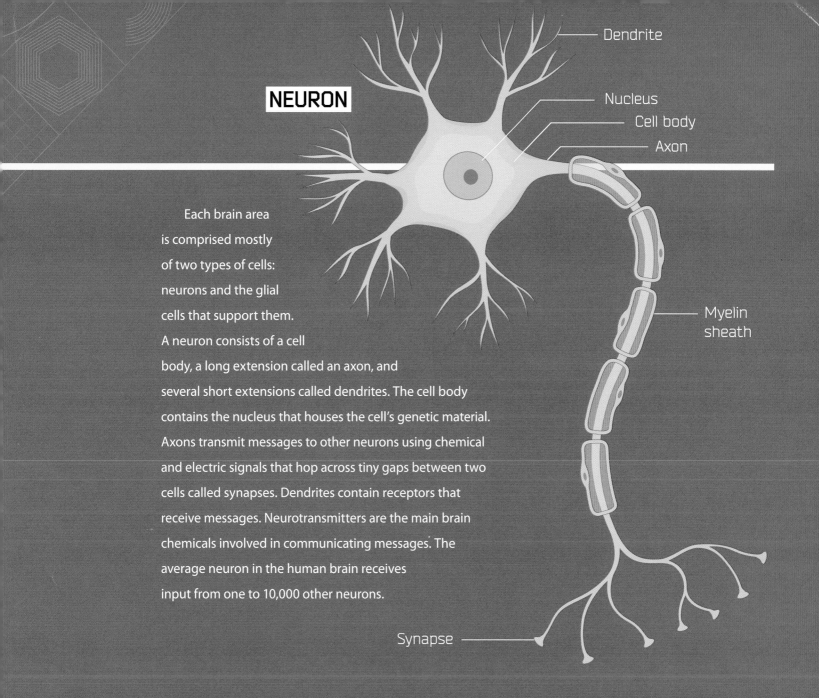

NEURON

Dendrite

Nucleus

Cell body

Axon

Myelin sheath

Synapse

Each brain area is comprised mostly of two types of cells: neurons and the glial cells that support them. A neuron consists of a cell body, a long extension called an axon, and several short extensions called dendrites. The cell body contains the nucleus that houses the cell's genetic material. Axons transmit messages to other neurons using chemical and electric signals that hop across tiny gaps between two cells called synapses. Dendrites contain receptors that receive messages. Neurotransmitters are the main brain chemicals involved in communicating messages. The average neuron in the human brain receives input from one to 10,000 other neurons.

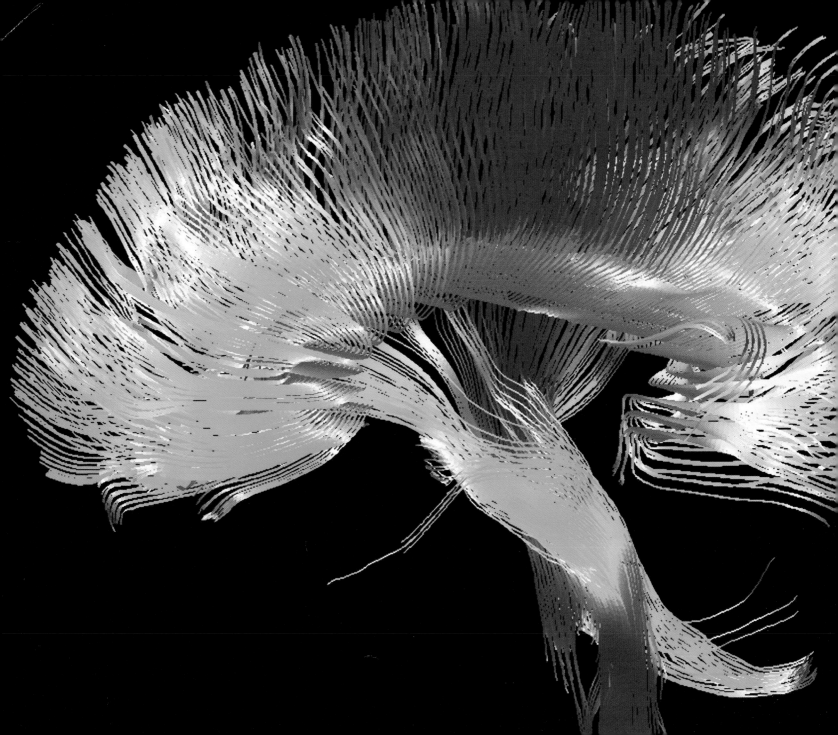

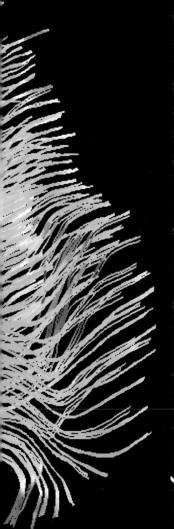

TWO

MAPPING THE
BRAIN

Numerous brain-mapping projects were underway by 2015. Some researchers sought to map animal brains, while others created wiring diagrams of the human brain. These efforts involved relatively new areas of science called neuroinformatics and connectomics. Neuroinformatics uses computer and mathematical models to organize and understand brain structure and function. Connectomics involves making wiring diagrams of the brain that follow neural connections.

The science of neuroinformatics originated in 1991, after several federal mental health and science agencies in the United States issued a report on the need to apply new mathematical, information-processing, and computer modeling technologies to neuroscience. Numerous researchers were awarded grants to pursue relevant research. Over the next several years, neuroinformatics agencies were founded in Europe and other parts of the world as well. Neuroinformatics projects allow neuroscientists

Mapping pathways in the brain may unlock a deeper understanding of the brain's functions.

to create theoretical models of nervous-system operations to guide their research and help them analyze research data.

Mapping the connections between the brain's billions of neurons is an incredibly challenging task.

The field of connectomics emerged more recently. Olaf Sporns of Indiana University and Patric Hagmann at Lausanne University in France each independently introduced the term *connectome* in 2005 to refer to a brain map. Sporns and his colleagues proposed mapping the human connectome to advance brain research. They noted, "To understand the functioning of a network, one must know its elements and their interconnections."[1] In his doctoral thesis, Hagmann determined imaging techniques, such as diffusion MRI, which tracks the movement of water molecules to trace neural connections, could be used to create a connectome of the brain.

Brain-Mapping Techniques

Some current brain-mapping projects, such as the Human Connectome Project being conducted at Washington University, the University of Minnesota, Massachusetts General Hospital, and the University of

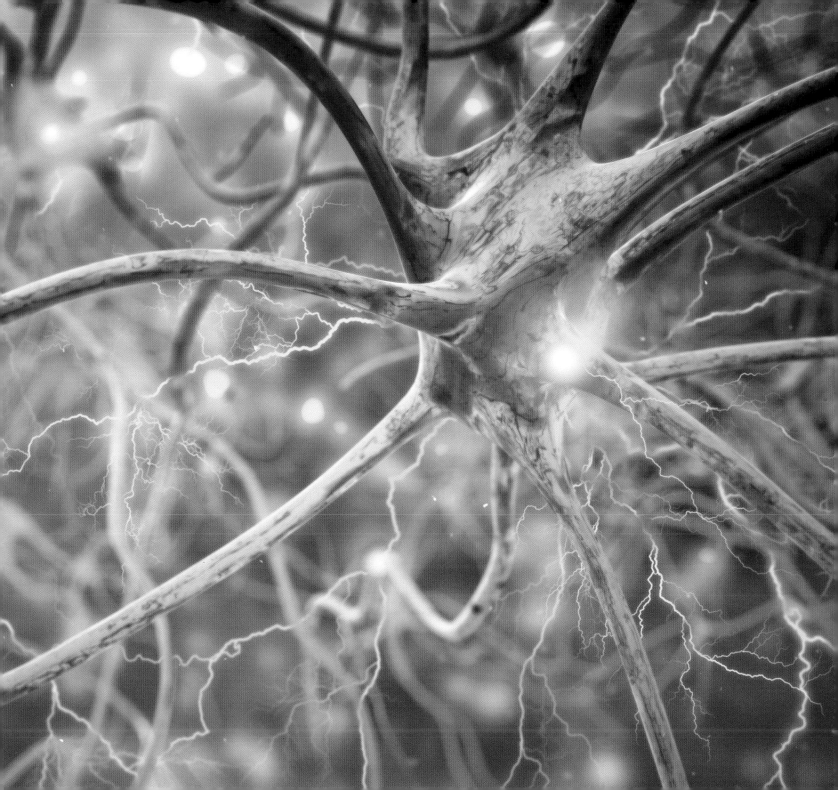

California, Los Angeles, are using diffusion MRI. This method takes advantage of the fact that the flow of water molecules in the brain is influenced by features of the surrounding tissue, including brain cells. Tracing patterns made by the water molecules reveals details about the structure of certain brain areas. Physicist Michio Kaku explains, "Since water follows the neural pathways of the brain, DTI [diffusion MRI] yields beautiful pictures that resemble networks of vines growing in a garden."[2] Doctors use the technique to plan operations to remove brain tumors.

Diffusion MRI technology can give doctors incredible views inside living brain tissue.

Another brain-mapping technique uses electron microscopes to view and photograph neurons in thin slices of brain tissue. The tissue is stained with fluorescent dyes to highlight neurons and other features. Electron microscopes are equipped with sophisticated computer systems that scan and combine the data from each tissue slice. Most brain-mapping projects use this technique.

The scale of brain-mapping projects is illustrated by the fact that only one complete brain has been mapped. The brain belongs to a nematode worm called *Caenorhabditis elegans*, which has 302 neurons and approximately 7,000 synapses. The project began in 1974, and researchers spent more than a decade assembling the first draft. Mapping the brains of

◢ The *Caenorhabditis elegans* Brain Map

In 1974, scientists led by Nobel Prize winner Sydney Brenner began mapping the first complete brain circuit, belonging to the worm *Caenorhabditis elegans*. They used a technique called serial electron microscopy. This technique involves slicing a brain into thin sheets and photographing all the neurons in each sheet with an electron microscope. The researchers kept track of the images manually, since computers at the time could not quickly process photographs. Based on the images, they constructed a map of all the neural connections. In 1986, Brenner and John White published a 341-page study detailing their findings. Although sections of other animals' brains have been mapped since then, no other complete maps have been made.

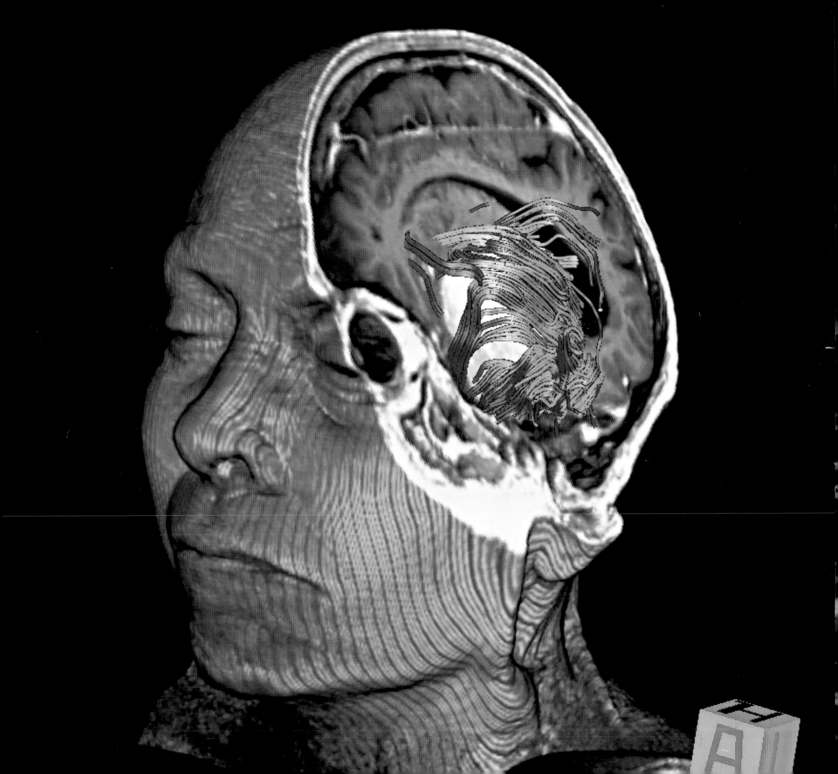

Fluorescent proteins reveal the neurons within Caenorhabditis elegans.

organisms with larger and more complex brains is a major undertaking, even with sophisticated computer programs and other modern technologies.

BOINC

Because of the time and expense involved with conventional brain-mapping methods, scientists led by Anthony Zador of Cold Spring Harbor Laboratory in New York pioneered a unique approach to mapping the mouse brain. The rodent's brain contains approximately 70 million neurons and

The ENIGMA Project

The world's largest brain-mapping project, ENIGMA, is headed by Arthur Toga and Paul Thompson of the University of Southern California. Using high-tech computers, gene sequencing, and brain-imaging tools, ENIGMA is answering important questions about brain function and malfunction. For example, combining data from 190 research centers around the world has helped Toga and Thompson trace how the human brain grows. This information has enhanced their understanding of how mental diseases, such as schizophrenia, develop. Toga and Thompson discovered the back parts of an infant's brain grow rapidly and establish many new neuron connections as the senses of vision and touch develop. Areas associated with language grow quickly as babies learn to speak. During adolescence, the most growth occurs in the front of the brain, which is linked to decision-making. As the front of the brain grows, other areas shrink to retain the brain's overall size. However, people who develop schizophrenia lose brain tissue much faster than normal during adolescence. Toga and Thompson's findings can help scientists develop new treatments.

100 billion synapses.[3] Zador's team uses gene-sequencing techniques, DNA barcodes, and a virus that hops from neuron to neuron to create a map of neural connections. The method is known as Barcoding of Individual Neuron Connections (BOINC).

Zador's gene-sequencing techniques trace connections among neurons by assigning each neuron a unique barcode. Usually, gene sequencing is used to create a map, known as the genome, of all the genes in an organism's DNA. Scientists collect a DNA sample and use one of several sequencing techniques to decipher the genome. Instead of signifying the cost of a product like conventional barcodes do, Zador's barcodes represent the unique DNA sequence in each neuron. Once each neuron is assigned a barcode, the researchers trace its connections to other neurons using a pseudorabies virus. The virus is useful for tracing neural connections because it infects mammals' brains by hopping from neuron to neuron. However, it has never been used to map an entire brain or to transport barcodes. The Cold Spring Harbor researchers have genetically engineered the virus DNA to include a neuron barcode. When the virus enters a new neuron, it brings in the barcodes from the previous neurons it has visited. Each neuron the virus infects contains its own barcode, plus copies of the barcodes of the neurons to which it is connected.

Sequencing Barcodes

After the virus has traced the brain's neural connections and placed barcodes inside each neuron, the researchers join the barcodes in a particular neuron into a single piece of DNA. Then, they use gene-sequencing to analyze the resulting DNA. This allows researchers to document all of the connections each neuron makes.

The researchers have succeeded in making each step of the procedure work by itself, but there are several technical issues to resolve before BOINC is up and running. One issue involves ensuring each barcode only crosses into the next neuron in the neural circuit. As a *Scientific American* article puts it, "Zador must ensure that these viral DNA barcodes have one-way, single-ride tickets—that they make only one hop and then stop."[4] Another issue is that the team must devise methods of determining which neurons are sending signals and which are receiving them based on the barcodes that end up inside them. Once these and several other issues are overcome, the team says their technique "could transform neuroscience research."[5]

DNA Barcodes

A

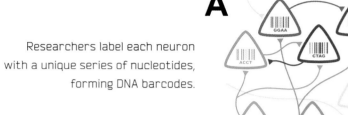

Researchers label each neuron with a unique series of nucleotides, forming DNA barcodes.

ATCG

In BOINC barcoding, each neuron is labeled with a unique DNA barcode. Barcodes from neurons that are connected by synapses are associated by carrying each other's barcode. The barcodes are then joined to create a brain map. The letters A, T, G, and C on each barcode represent the base chemicals that make up the nucleotides, or chemical building blocks, that comprise each DNA molecule. *A* stands for adenine, *T* for thymine, *G* for guanine, and *C* for cytosine.

B

Each neuron contains the DNA barcodes from the neurons to which it is connected.

C

The DNA barcodes within each neuron are joined into pairs based on which neurons are connected to it.

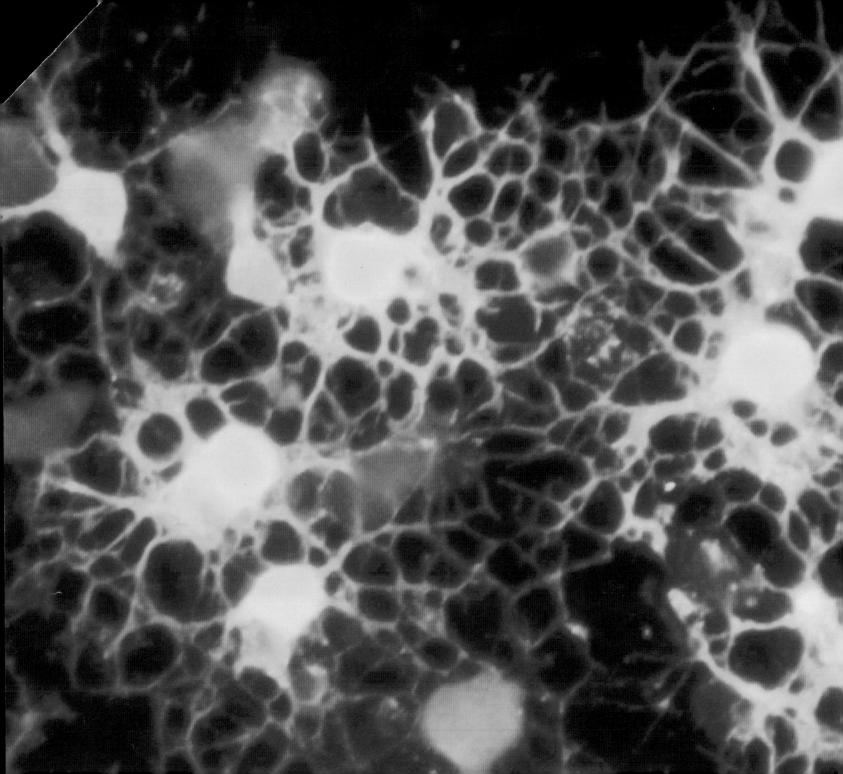

THREE

A SEE-THROUGH
BRAIN

Scientists hope to develop methods of clearly viewing intact, three-dimensional brains. Studying the brain during an autopsy requires cutting up tissue into thin slices, which prevents investigators from seeing the whole inside of the brain at once. And even though imaging methods, such as MRI, allow scientists to see inside the brain, the view is still obscured, mostly by lipids, or fat molecules. Lipids prevent light and chemicals that can highlight cells and other structures from getting inside the brain.

In 2013, researchers led by Karl Deisseroth at Stanford University created a transparent mouse brain using a technique called CLARITY. This technique involves chemical engineering and neuroscience technologies. CLARITY helps scientists see and map neural circuits, thus fulfilling the hope for viewing the entire inside of the brain, along with its molecular parts. CLARITY brains are viewed by shining lights into the structure and using dyes that highlight certain areas. As Deisseroth explains, "To be able to see

New technologies are making it possible to get clearer views than ever before of brains and the cells that make them up.

Types of Neurons

Scientists know there are hundreds of neuron types, many of which have not yet been identified. CLARITY has helped neuroscientists identify different kinds of neurons and promises to continue enhancing knowledge in this area.

Neuroscientists usually classify neurons into three main types based on their function. Sensory neurons send signals from sense organs to the brain. Motor neurons transmit signals from the brain and spinal cord to the muscles. Interneurons connect sensory and motor neurons.

Sometimes, neurons are classified by shape. They can be pyramid, star, or cone shaped. Other times, their classification depends on which neurotransmitter chemical they contain.

Another way to classify neurons is by the number of dendrites they contain. Unipolar neurons have one dendrite, bipolar neurons have two, and multipolar neurons have more than two.

the fine detail and the big picture at the same time . . . has been a major unmet goal that CLARITY begins to address."[1] The Stanford team developed CLARITY using brains from deceased mice but has shown the technique works on other animals' brains and on other organs as well.

Developing CLARITY

Deisseroth and his colleagues figured out a way to remove lipid molecules from the brain while leaving brain cells and structures intact. They used chemical engineering to replace lipids with a transparent hydrogel, a gel-like substance that contains mostly water. The researchers built the hydrogel from molecules within the brain called hydrogel monomers. The hydrogel sticks to all neural molecules except lipids. The researchers placed a mouse brain into a container filled with the hydrogel. It took approximately two days for the brain to soak up the gel. Once it did, the gel gave structure and support to all the brain tissue.

The researchers then used a technique called electrophoresis to extract the lipids. Electrophoresis involves separating molecules based on their size, density, or purity. It is often used to separate and

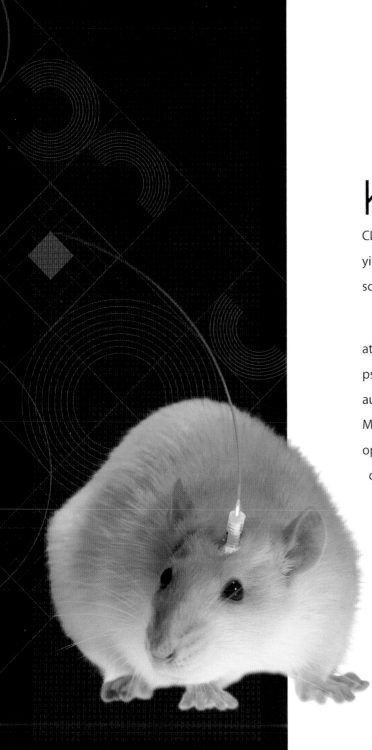

Karl **Deisseroth**
(1971–)

Karl Deisseroth is well known for his groundbreaking contributions to neuroscience, particularly his pioneering work on optogenetics and CLARITY. Optogenetics, involving the use of light-sensitive proteins, has yielded significant insight into the causes of illnesses such as depression, schizophrenia, and Parkinson's disease.

As a professor of bioengineering, psychiatry, and behavioral sciences at Stanford University, Deisseroth teaches, does research, and practices psychiatric medicine, primarily treating patients with depression and autism. He has won numerous awards for his work, including the 2010 Method of the Year award from the journal *Nature Methods* for pioneering optogenetics and the 2015 Lurie Prize in Biomedical Sciences for the development of optogenetics and CLARITY. He told the scientific journal *Nature* he developed these techniques because he realized doctors had few tools to help them explain the biological causes of psychiatric illnesses. "It was extremely clear that for fundamental advances in these domains I would have to spend time developing new tools," he said.[2]

Deisseroth and his team created a system that uses lasers to stop tremors in mice suffering from Parkinson's disease.

identify proteins or DNA in a mixture or blood sample. The procedure involves applying an electric charge to a substance in a solution. The solution is inside a container with a positively charged and a negatively charged electrode. The electric jolt causes molecules in the solution to start moving. Negatively charged molecules are naturally attracted to the positively charged electrode, and positively charged molecules are attracted to the negatively charged electrode. Deisseroth's team used the electric charge to move lipids out of the brain. Within a few days, all the lipid molecules were gone, leaving the brain transparent. The entire process of making a brain transparent using CLARITY takes approximately two weeks.

Dyeing cells is a common way of viewing the tiny structures within them.

CLARITY Applications

CLARITY allows scientists to view and photograph brain structures, cells, and neural pathways using electron microscopes and various dyes. It also lets them gather information about how chemicals interact with brain structures and each other. To do this, researchers use fluorescent antibodies. Antibodies are chemicals that seek and attach themselves to specific proteins. Fluorescent antibodies contain substances that glow when exposed to light. Scientists use them to determine the types of proteins present in each brain area.

Scientists can inject dyes that bind to specific brain cell types. This lets them identify which brain cells are present in particular brain areas and study how these cells connect to other cells. The Stanford team discovered a CLARITY brain can be reused for many such studies. Researchers can flush out the dyes and study the brain again with different dyes.

Scientists have already used CLARITY to gain knowledge about the biological causes of drug addiction, Alzheimer's disease, and several other neurological disorders. For example, researchers at

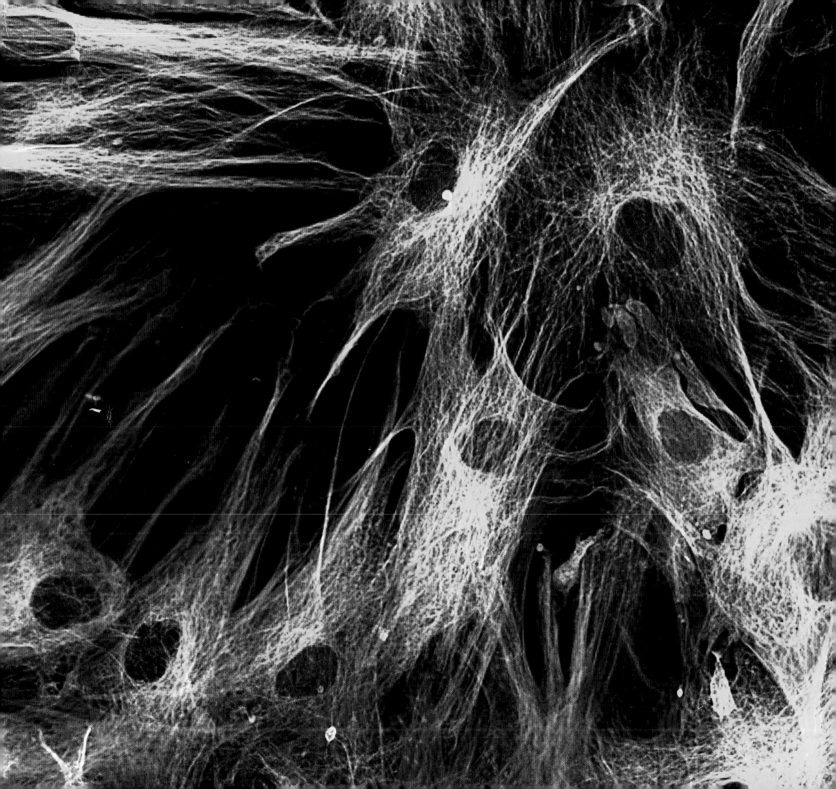

A. The brain of a normal elderly person

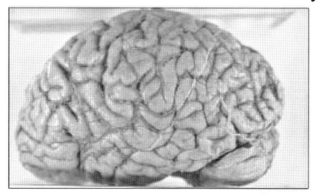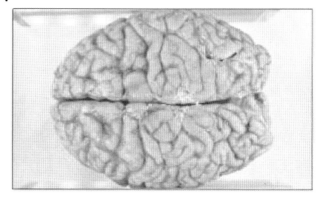

B. The brain of a person with Alzheimer's disease

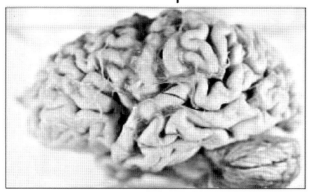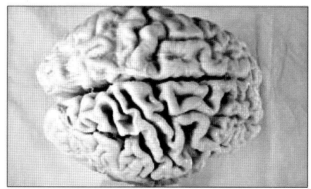

C. The brain of a person with alcoholism

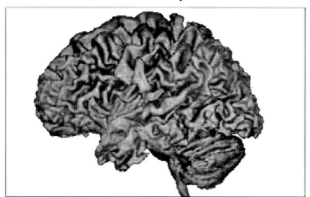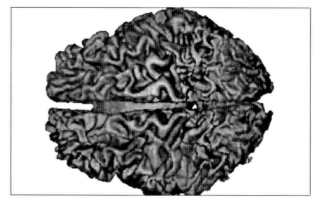

Alzheimer's disease and addictive drugs can have severe effects on the brain.

hospitals in Toronto, Canada, used CLARITY to study the biological mechanisms underlying cocaine addiction. Scientists have known for a long time that cocaine produces long-lasting memories called cocaine engrams that contribute to addiction. However, they did not know where these memories were encoded and stored. Using CLARITY, the researchers found certain neurons in a part of the limbic system called the amygdala became active when cocaine was administered. The amygdala is especially important in processing emotions, such as fear and pleasure, and in coordinating emotions and memory.

The neurons that were active while the engram formed contained high levels of a transcription factor called CREB. Transcription factors are chemicals that bind to certain genes and activate them. CREB regulates activity in genes that oversee the formation of long-term memories. When these genes are active, new connections form between neurons. CREB plays a big role in drug addiction. When the researchers disabled neurons with high levels of CREB, the cocaine engram did not develop.

◢ What Is Alzheimer's Disease?

Alzheimer's disease is one of the most devastating types of dementia. It usually affects elderly people, though it can strike earlier in life. Fifty percent of Americans over age 80 develop Alzheimer's, and because people are living longer, it is one of the fastest-growing diseases.[3] Alzheimer's involves the progressive breakdown of memory and other brain functions. At first, short-term memory is affected. As the disease continues, many patients cannot recognize family members or care for themselves. Researchers have identified some of the underlying brain changes that accompany Alzheimer's. Cognitive reserve, aided by a healthy diet and exercise, can delay the onset of the disease. However, once it is diagnosed, there are no effective treatments. Many research projects, including those using CLARITY, are seeking to discover methods of preventing and curing this disease.

The connection between CREB and memory was previously established by research that found activating CREB in fruit flies results in them learning and remembering tasks ten times faster than normal flies. In contrast, fruit flies given an extra gene that represses CREB cannot form memories. However, until CLARITY demonstrated the formation of cocaine engrams, no one tied CREB to drug addiction, and no one knew why many former cocaine addicts experience renewed cravings when exposed to an environment in which they previously used cocaine. The researchers now think the engram contains memories of this environment, which are triggered by being there at a later time. They believe these findings may lead to new types of drug addiction treatments.

The Future of CLARITY

Since CLARITY is so new, scientists are not yet sure how long transparent CLARITY brains can be stored or how long the transparency will last. They also do not know if the CLARITY process can be repeated to make a brain reusable once a brain's transparency decays. But even with these unanswered questions, experts say CLARITY will revolutionize neuroscience. As Thomas Insel, director of the National Institute of Mental Health, states, CLARITY "promises to transform the way we study the brain's anatomy and how disease changes it. No longer will the in-depth study of our most important three-dimensional organ be constrained by two-dimensional methods."[4]

Some studies have already been done using CLARITY on human brain tissue. Doctors are exploring the possibility of using CLARITY to help diagnose various diseases in the rest of the body, including cancer, infections, and autoimmune disorders, diseases in which the immune system attacks the body. This cutting-edge technology's applications may extend far beyond its ability to revolutionize neuroscience.

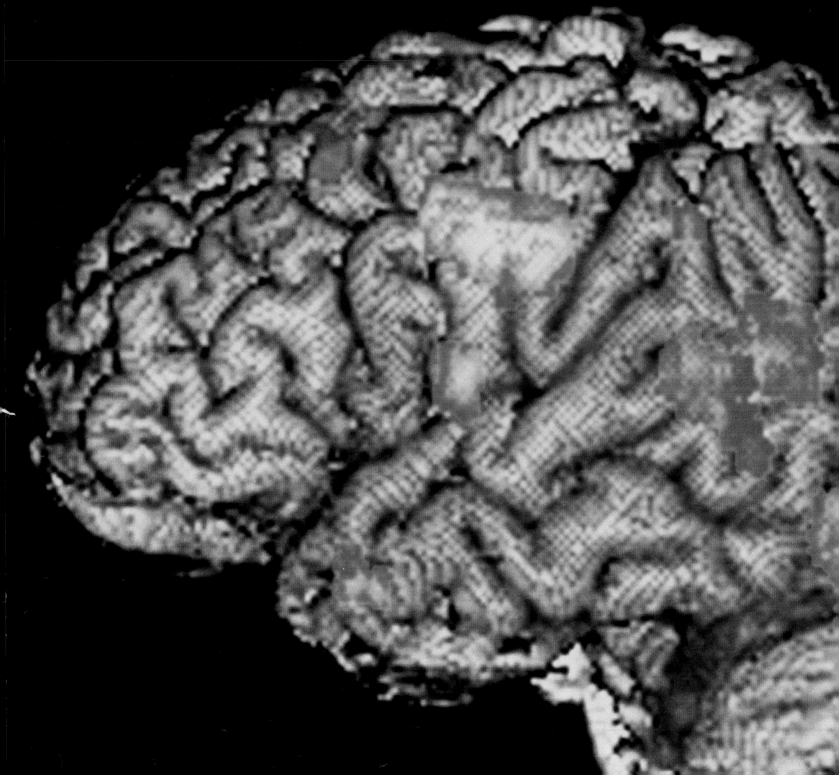

FOUR

TRACING COMMON ROOTS OF BRAIN DISORDERS

New research reveals many mental illnesses share the same brain abnormalities. For the first time, scientists have associated common biological causes with multiple brain disorders. There are two basic categories of brain disorders. Functional disorders impact the way the brain functions, whereas organic disorders affect the physical structure of the brain. Doctors know complex interactions between genes and a person's environment lead to the brain abnormalities that cause most mental illnesses. However, researchers had not previously studied how these diverse factors can result in similar brain abnormalities. As the authors of a 2015 study led by Gerome Breen of Kings College London and Peter Holmans of Cardiff University note, "There is an urgent need to clearly identify the biological mechanisms and pathways underlying risk."[1]

Brain scans show which parts of the brain are active during schizophrenic hallucinations.

Psychiatry and Neurology

Psychiatry and neurology are separate medical specialties, though they share much in common. Neurological diseases were traditionally regarded as stemming from biological abnormalities in the nervous system, while psychiatric disorders were mainly associated with emotional and social problems. With more and more research proving mental diseases are caused by brain abnormalities, the distinctions between psychiatry and neurology have become blurred. Multiple sclerosis, for instance, results from the immune system damaging the fatty covering around nerve axons. This can cause vision loss, pain, and impaired coordination. It also causes behavioral changes, including mood problems and depression.

Researchers involved in the study led by Breen and Holmans examined the genomes of more than 60,000 people with schizophrenia, bipolar disorder, or major depressive disorder.[2] Schizophrenia is characterized by severe thought distortions. It may involve an inability to distinguish reality from fantasy. Emotional problems are central to bipolar disorder, which involves dramatic mood swings. Major depressive disorder is characterized by severe depression.

The researchers used computer software that tracks the biological effects of gene mutations. A mutation is a change in the genetic sequence of an organism's DNA. It can be caused by outside forces, such as chemicals, or by natural processes, such as errors that occur when DNA makes copies of itself. The researchers uncovered patterns showing how different mutations associated with various diseases all lead to abnormal neuron communications. Many of the abnormalities result from disruptions in the flow of calcium into the neurons. Calcium is known to be important in many brain processes, such as learning and memory. For example, when calcium flows into neurons while an individual is learning a new subject, it strengthens connections between the neurons. It does this by intensifying the electric

Calcium plays an important role in the synapses between neurons.

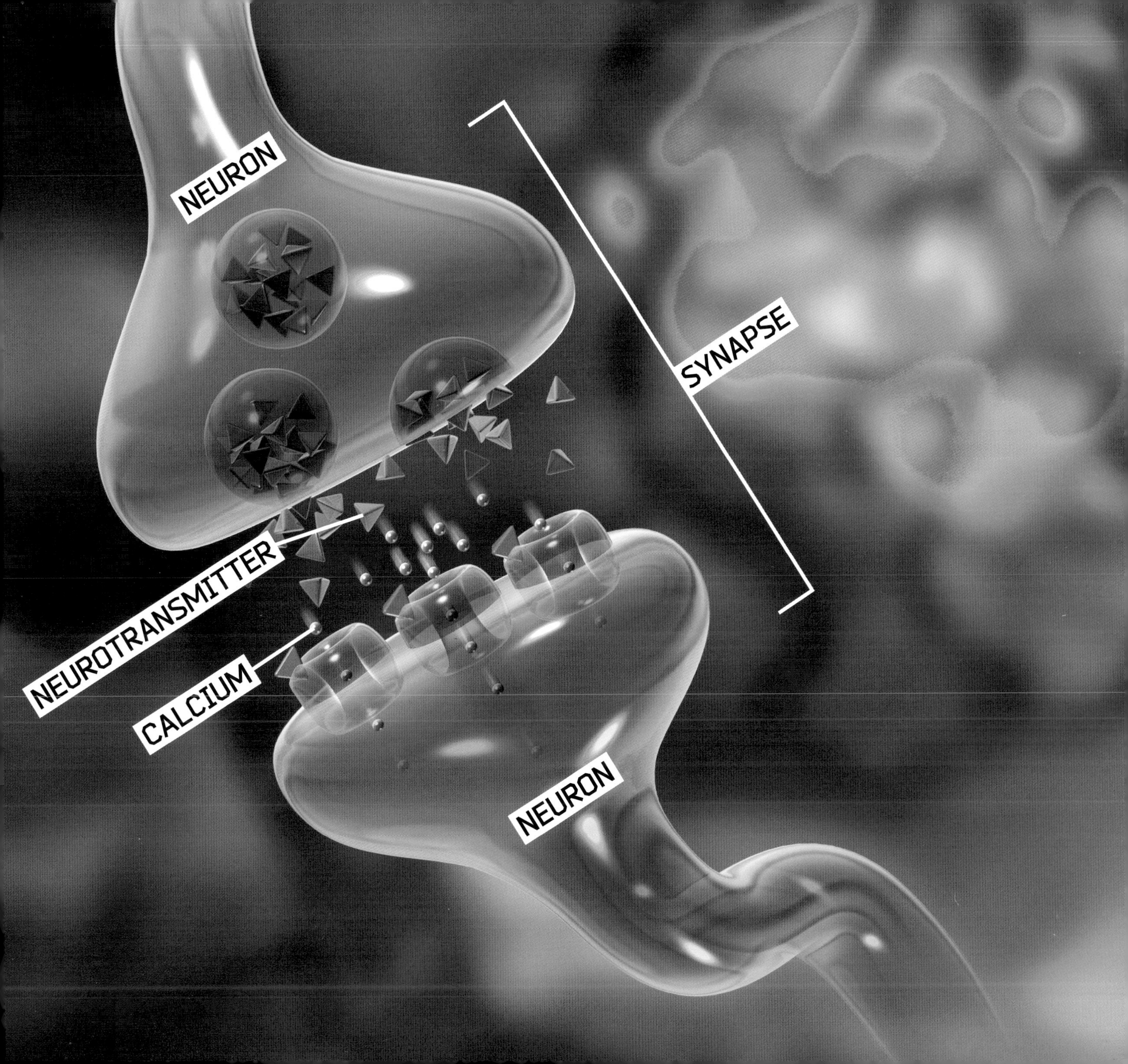
NEURON
SYNAPSE
NEUROTRANSMITTER
CALCIUM
NEURON

Abnormal Biochemistry

Two of the most prominent biochemical issues that increase the risk of mental disorders result from gene mutations that affect histone methylation and calcium channel activity. Histones are proteins found in DNA. Methylation occurs when a methyl group—a molecule made of carbon and hydrogen—sticks to a histone. This can inappropriately turn genes on or off, instructing cells to produce too much or too little of a protein. Incorrect amounts of proteins can cause a variety of diseases.

Calcium channels are tiny gates in cell membranes that regulate the passage of calcium from the bloodstream into and out of the cells. Calcium is important in regulating neural circuits involved in perception, learning, memory, and thinking.

signals sent from one neuron to another. Disruptions in the flow of calcium can impair the ability to learn and remember.

Mutations also can lead to problems with the brain. Some mutations affect chemicals called histones, which turn genes on or off to regulate brain-cell production of the proteins needed for brain development. Without the correct amount of these proteins, a variety of brain abnormalities can occur.

Interneurons and Brain Disorders

Research published in March 2015 by Paul Worley at the Johns Hopkins School of Medicine sheds light on other common causes underlying different mental disorders and builds on previous work on interneurons. Neuroscientists often liken interneurons to orchestra conductors. The cells ensure all the neurons in a brain circuit are firing at the appropriate times to keep the brain and its signals running smoothly. Interneurons normally become embedded in the brain during fetal development.

Scientists previously discovered malfunctioning interneurons contribute to illnesses such as Alzheimer's disease, epilepsy, anxiety disorders, and schizophrenia. Worley's research indicates that when a certain type of interneuron does not embed into neural networks during brain development, the brain does not establish normal signaling patterns. This can lead to the development of mental disorders later in life. The precise disease that develops depends largely on an individual's gene abnormalities.

Worley discovered two proteins known as pentraxins are key to allowing interneurons to properly integrate into neural networks during fetal development in mice. Pentraxins are proteins that recognize chemical patterns on cell surfaces. They affect the proteins on the surface of interneurons, making interneurons attractive to other types of neurons. The other neurons then form connections with the interneurons. Worley found interneurons in mice that are genetically engineered to lack pentraxins connect to other neurons much later than normal during fetal development. This prevents neurons in the hippocampus—a part of the brain involved in memory formation, among other functions—from establishing normal signaling patterns. The effects of abnormal signaling patterns often are not apparent until later in life, when the mice that lacked pentraxins developed impaired memory and, sometimes, anxiety, depression, or other psychiatric disorders. Worley believes this knowledge may lead to the development of drugs that target pentraxins to treat various types of disorders.

◢ Genes and Mental Illness Risk

Some illnesses, such as cystic fibrosis, are caused by a single gene mutation. For other diseases, a combination of many mutations increases the chance of developing the illness. Schizophrenia and autism fall into this category. In order for these diseases to develop, however, certain environmental factors, such as exposure to a particular virus before birth, must also be present. Then, the gene mutations and environmental factors can result in brain abnormalities that cause the disease.

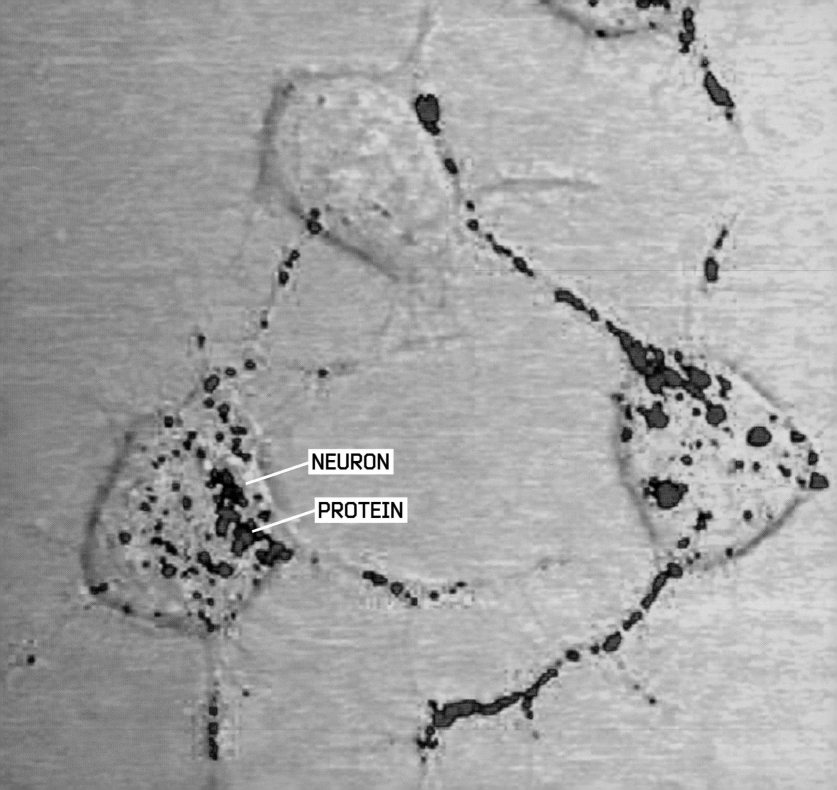

Attention Problems

Research by Bo Li at Cold Spring Harbor Laboratory sheds light on another brain mechanism involved in many brain disorders: an inability to filter incoming information. This inability leads to difficulties in focusing one's attention, which is common in diseases such as schizophrenia and attention deficit disorder. Indeed, many people with these diseases say they cannot focus their attention because of a confusing storm of unfiltered information. As schizophrenia expert E. Fuller Torrey explains in his book *Surviving Schizophrenia*, "It is difficult to concentrate or pay attention when so much sensory data are rushing through the brain."[3]

In a study reported in 2015 in *Nature Neuroscience*, Li's team found the brain circuit that filters irrelevant information and allows mice to concentrate on relevant information. This circuit is in the thalamic reticular nucleus (TRN), a layer of neurons that coats a part of the brain called the thalamus. As is the hippocampus, the thalamus is part of the limbic system. The thalamus regulates sleep, attention, and consciousness. It also functions as a gateway for signals from the sensory organs to the thought-processing centers in the cortex. The neurons of the TRN produce GABA, a chemical that reduces neuron activity. This type of chemical is known as an inhibitory neurotransmitter.

Defects Underlying Attention Problems

Before Li's research, neuroscientists knew people with damage to the TRN found it difficult to pay attention. Some experts suspected the TRN was responsible for filtering sensory information before the thalamus sent it to the cortex. No one, however, understood which types of neurons performed the filtering or how they accomplished this. Li's team used genetic engineering, fluorescent antibodies, and behavior tests to prove TRN neurons require a protein called ErbB4 to produce GABA and filter sensory information. The researchers engineered mice to lack ErbB4 and tested their behavior. One test required the mice to ignore background noises and focus on a visual cue. The ErbB4-deficient mice could not do this, while normal mice could. Li also noted, "When ErbB4 is absent, we saw that the connections between the cortex and the TRN become much stronger."[4] This demonstrated that when TRN was unable to filter the information it sent to the cortex, the signal traffic between the TRN and cortex increased dramatically.

The researchers noted many people with schizophrenia and other disorders involving attention problems are unable to properly regulate ErbB4. Neuroscientists believe this knowledge could lead to new types of medications to treat diverse mental disorders.

The thalamus may play a key role in helping people focus their attention.

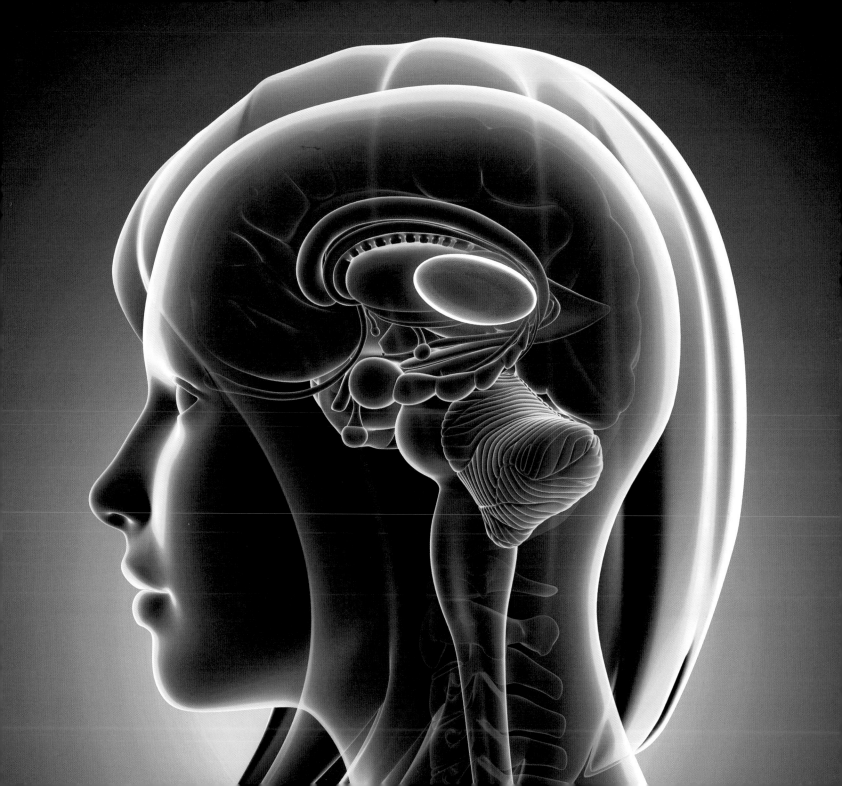

FIVE

BODY DEFENSES AND MENTAL ILLNESSES

For many years, doctors believed psychiatric illnesses were primarily caused by neurotransmitter imbalances that resulted from a combination of genetic and environmental causes. For example, most experts believed deficiencies in a neurotransmitter called serotonin caused depression. This is why most antidepressant medications increase the amount of serotonin in the brain. However, new research reveals the immune system also plays a big role, suggesting new treatment targets for these illnesses.

Antidepressant drugs, pink, regulate serotonin levels at the junctions between nerves.

The Immune System

The immune system is a collection of organs, tissues, and cells that defend against infections. The main cells involved are the many types of white blood cells, including lymphocytes, macrophages, and neutrophils. Some white blood cells produce chemicals called antibodies that recognize and fight invasive organisms and other foreign substances that enter the body. Other white blood cells produce chemicals called cytokines. They mobilize still other white blood cells and contribute to the inflammation that occurs when the immune system is active. Some types of white blood cells physically destroy invading microorganisms.

Scientists have discovered the brain has its own immune cells, called microglia. They act as sentries, patrolling the brain for possible danger. Microglia become active in response to infections or other threats to brain health. When activated, microglia gobble up germs and secrete cytokines. The cytokines cause the inflammation associated with depression and other mental disorders.

Depression and the Immune System

In January 2015, Jonathan Savitz at the Laureate Institute for Brain Research released a study that used MRI and brain-chemical analysis. It showed a link between the chemicals released in the brain in response to inflammation and brain characteristics of people with depression. When immune system activity results in inflammation, brain cells release neuroprotective chemicals. These chemicals protect the brain from harm. The brain cells also release neurotoxic chemicals that can harm neurons.

Savitz and his team studied a particular type of kynurenine metabolites that were either neurotoxic or neuroprotective. In other words, they were either harmful or helpful. Metabolites are by-products of chemical reactions in the body. The researchers found depressed people's brains have a higher ratio of neurotoxic kynurenine metabolites to neuroprotective kynurenine metabolites than nondepressed people's brains. Reduced neuroprotective chemicals correlates with reduced size in the hippocampus and amygdala, both of which are important in mood regulation. The researchers also found depressed

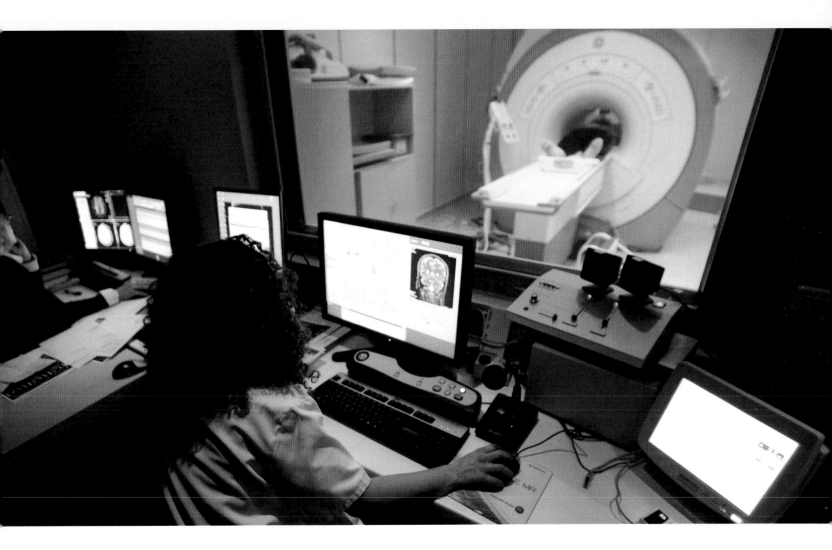

MRIs can reveal the impact of mental illnesses, such as depression, on the brain's chemistry.

people with very few neuroprotective kynurenine metabolites are more likely to have a serious symptom called anhedonia, an inability to feel pleasure.

Previous research showed severely depressed people have smaller-than-normal hippocampi and amygdalae. Other research showed inflammation in laboratory animals leads to depressed behavior and similar size reductions in these brain areas. Scientists discovered an immune chemical called interleukin-1 triggers the production of neurotoxic kynurenine metabolites. These damaging chemicals cause a loss of synapses, degraded dendrites, and neuron death. Such problems can lead to a smaller-than-normal hippocampus and amygdala. Savitz believes these findings also apply to depression in humans. He concludes that new types of antidepressant medications could aim to increase levels of neuroprotective kynurenine metabolites in the brain.

PET scans can reveal what is happening in multiple slices of a person's brain.

More Inflammation, More Depression

Related research reported in January 2015 by scientists at the University of Toronto used a new tissue dye and positron emission tomography (PET) scans to prove that among patients with major depressive disorder, more brain inflammation results in a worsened depression. The new dye also allowed researchers to detect increased levels of translocator proteins in brain areas that regulate mood. The presence of these proteins indicates neuron inflammation has taken place. Higher levels of translocator proteins correlate with more severe depression. This was the first time scientists found a marker of brain inflammation in people with depression.

The researchers also found that a type of glia known as microglia, which function as immune cells in the brain, are active in the brains of depressed people. This suggests new drugs to treat depression might aim to decrease microglia activity. Studies on laboratory rodents proved an antibiotic called minocycline hydrochloride, which reduces microglia activity, reduced symptoms of depression. However, the researchers pointed out that just because brain inflammation and depression occur together, it does not necessarily mean one causes the other. Further research is needed to confirm whether this is the case. Still, the Toronto researchers suggest their study "provides the most

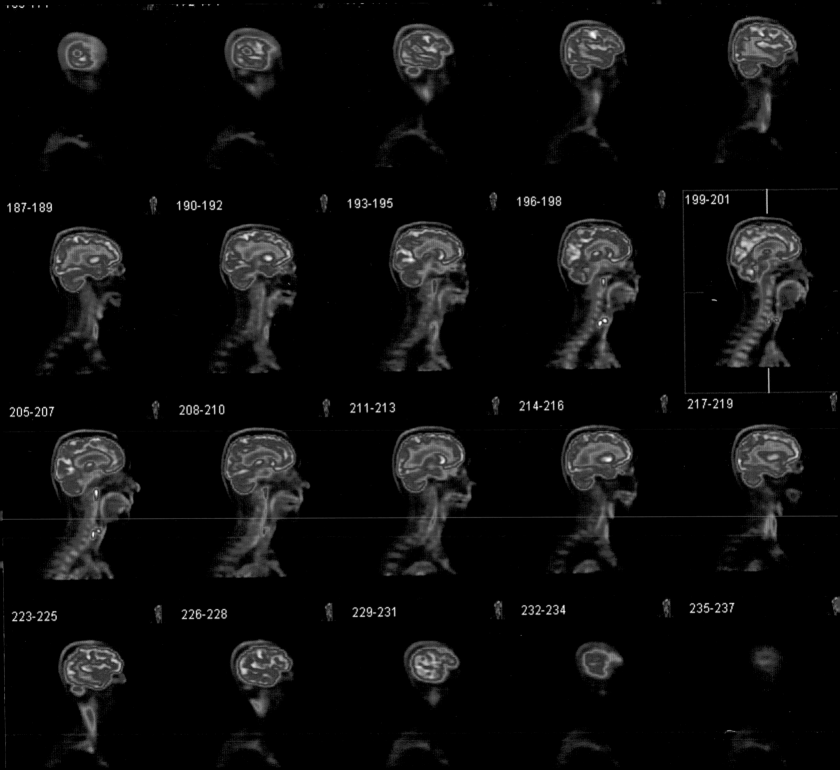

compelling evidence to date of brain inflammation" playing a big role in major depression.[1]

Some PTSD treatments involve using virtual reality to relive traumatic experiences.

Post-Traumatic Stress Disorder and the Immune System

Other research indicates the immune system plays a role in causing a mental disorder called post-traumatic stress disorder (PTSD). People with PTSD experience terrifying flashbacks to traumatic events, such as war or abuse. Many soldiers who survive horrific battle injuries or see their fellow soldiers killed develop PTSD. However, not all people who experience traumas are affected by the disorder.

One study involving US marines found activity in certain genes that regulate the immune system can reliably predict who will or will not develop PTSD after serving in combat. Researchers led by Ming Tsuang of the University of California, San Diego, discovered susceptibility to developing PTSD is determined by genes in white blood cells that control the innate immune system and the release of a protein called interferon. The innate immune system is the body's first line of defense against invading germs, becoming active immediately after germs enter the body. It launches immune cells and chemicals that attack the germs.

A COLLECTION |

ent VFX

Insurgents Appear

Insurgents Disappear

Civilian VFX

Waving Child

Child Disappear

IED VFX

Detonate Ambulances

Reset Ambulances

◢ Stress and Depression

Doctors know people who react strongly to stress are at higher risk for depression. However, they do not know why this is true. Studies at the Icahn School of Medicine provide clues about this question and shed light on the relationship between depression and the immune system. A research team found some people and mice are genetically wired to develop depression when stressed, while others are resilient to stress. Immune cells in susceptible animals and people release large amounts of a cytokine called interleukin-6 (IL-6) before, during, and after stressful situations. Furthermore, people with major depression who have high levels of IL-6 generally do not experience reduced depression when given antidepressant drugs. The researchers found blocking IL-6 in susceptible mice makes them behave more like the resilient mice. They believe this finding may help scientists develop new treatments for depression that involve targeting IL-6.

The researchers used gene-sequencing techniques to discover that the genes controlling the innate immune system and those controlling the release of interferon were overactive in marines with PTSD. On the other hand, marines without PTSD showed increased activity in genes that stimulate healing after an injury. All the marines received blood tests both before and after being deployed to a war zone. The results were the same both times. Experts believe this knowledge may soon lead to a test to identify people who are vulnerable to PTSD.

Research on the brains and immune systems of PTSD sufferers may improve care for people involved in traumatic events.

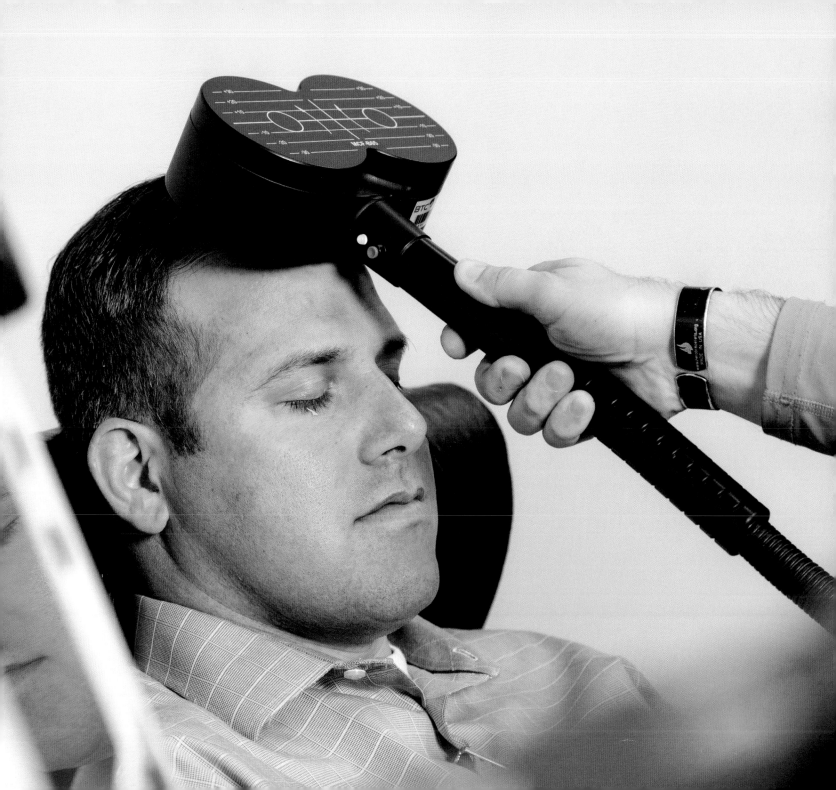

SIX

THE FORGOTTEN CELLS

For many years, scientists thought neurons were the key players in the brain. When glia, the other type of brain cells, were first described in the 1800s, experts thought they merely supported neurons by bringing nutrients and adding structure to connect parts of the brain. When German doctor Rudolf Virchow named glia cells in 1856, he called them *nervenkitt*, which means "nerve glue" in German. The word *nervenkitt* was later translated into neuroglia in English. Today, the cells are referred to as glia or glial cells.

Recent studies indicate glia do not just serve as nerve glue but instead are as important as neurons. One of the first clues about their importance came from Johns Hopkins University neuroscientist Marian Diamond in 1985. Studying the brain of deceased physicist Albert Einstein, she found its prefrontal and parietal cortexes contained a higher ratio of glial cells to neurons than normal. These areas of the brain are important in decision-making and problem solving. Einstein was

Virchow made a wide variety of discoveries about many aspects of the human body.

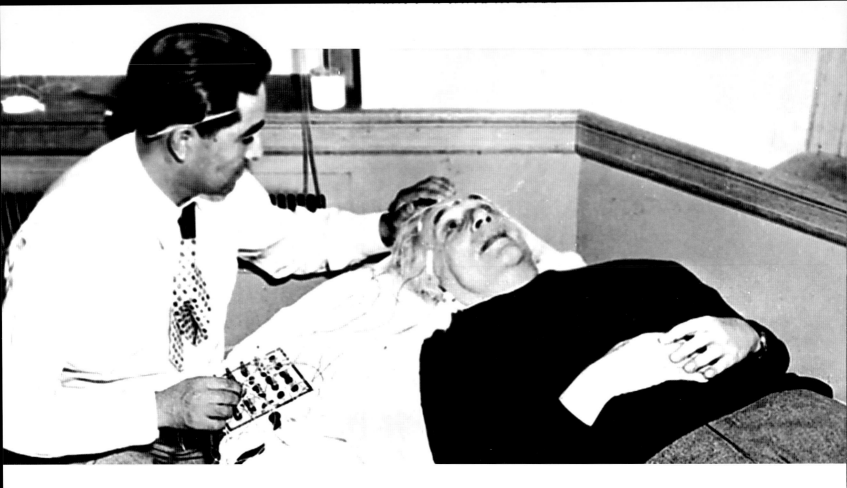

During and after his life, Einstein's brain was of intense interest.

considered one of the most intelligent humans who ever lived. After he died in 1955, scientists removed his brain and preserved it in a jar of formaldehyde. Many researchers requested slices of his brain to study in hopes of determining what made him so smart.

What Do Glia Do?

Other researchers later pinpointed many ways in which glia are critical for brain function. In fact, glia are so important that National Institutes of Health neuroscientist R. Douglas Fields believes the

BRAIN initiative's emphasis on mapping neuron connections "is unlikely to deliver the promised benefits—which include understanding perception, consciousness, how the brain produces memories, and the development of treatments for diseases such as epilepsy, depression and schizophrenia" unless glia also are mapped.[1] Fields and other researchers discovered that glia sense and control neuron activity and play a big role in brain injuries and diseases.

Although glia do not produce electric signals as neurons do, they communicate with each other and with neurons using neurotransmitters and other chemicals sent through gap junctions. Gap junctions are tiny channels that allow cells to connect to other cells. Similar to disruptions in synapses, disruptions in gap junction communications can cause brain diseases.

The precise functions of glia depend on their type. The three major types are oligodendrocytes, microglia, and astrocytes.

◢ Einstein's Brain

Many scientists studied Albert Einstein's preserved brain after his death in hopes of discovering what made him a genius. In 1999, researchers at McMaster University in Canada found Einstein's parietal lobes were 15 percent wider than normal.[2] They believe this may have contributed to his remarkable ability to understand mathematics and physics. The scientists also noted Einstein's brain was smaller overall than normal but had more grooves and ridges in the cortex, giving it more surface area. In 2009, anthropologist Dean Falk discovered an unusual knob-like structure in an area of Einstein's motor cortex that controls the left hand. Similar structures have been found in the brains of people with musical talent. Einstein was a talented violinist from childhood. No one has proved these brain features directly resulted in Einstein's specific capabilities, but it seems likely they played a role.

Oligodendrocytes

Oligodendrocytes produce myelin, the fatty substance that forms a sheath around axons. The myelin sheath works like insulation around an electric wire, allowing electric signals to quickly travel along axons. Without myelin, a neuron's electric signal slows down or is completely blocked. This is what happens in patients with multiple sclerosis (MS). MS results from an individual's immune system destroying myelin. The disease is characterized by the loss of many abilities, such as walking, seeing, or thinking, depending on which brain areas are affected. As Fields explains, MS is disabling because "nervous system function depends on information being transmitted at high speed."[3]

Scientists thought another type of glia called astrocytes were the main glia involved in learning and memory, but a 2014 study at University College London indicated oligodendrocytes are also critical to these brain functions. The study found genetically engineered mice unable to produce myelin could not learn a new task. Those that could produce myelin were able to learn the task.

Astrocytes

The role of astrocytes—named for their starlike shape—in learning and memory has been studied extensively. Astrocytes regulate neuron growth, synapse formation, and synapse activity. In fact, a single astrocyte can influence activity in 2 million synapses in the human brain.[4] Since learning and memory depend on what is known as synaptic plasticity, astrocytes play a huge role in these brain functions. Synaptic plasticity is the ability of brain cells to change their connections and signaling patterns in response to a person or animal's experiences. This allows the brain to build more efficient connections over time. Astrocytes regulate synaptic activity by adjusting the concentration of calcium, potassium, and other substances. Astrocytes also play a role in producing neurotransmitters.

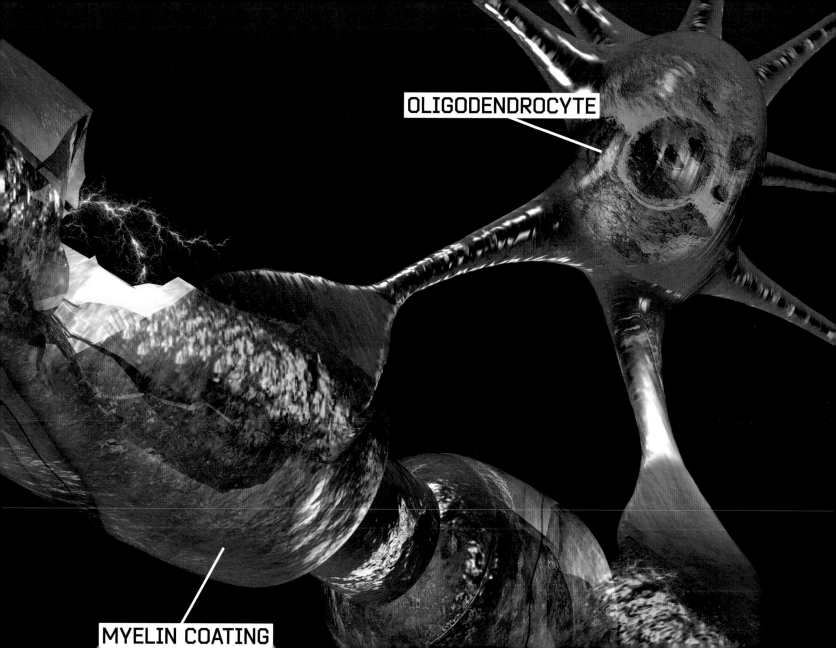

Half-Human, Half-Mouse Brains

Many people questioned if the University of Rochester project that injected human astrocytes into mouse brains made the mice partially human. However, lead researcher Steve Goldman stated, "It's still a mouse brain, not a human brain. . . . This does not provide the animals with additional capabilities that could in any way be ascribed or perceived as specifically human. Rather, the human cells are simply improving the efficiency of the mouse's own neural networks."[7] Goldman pointed out the smart mice still behaved like mice, socializing with other mice and displaying other typical mouse behaviors.

Another ethical issue arose when the researchers considered performing similar experiments on monkeys, which are much more closely related to humans. However, Goldman stated they "decided not to because of all the potential ethical issues."[8] German neuroscientist Wolfgang Enard expressed the ethical dilemma when he commented, "If you make animals more human-like, where do you stop?"[9]

They are particularly involved in the production of glutamate. Astrocytes produce a chemical called glutamine, which is needed to produce glutamate. Researchers have discovered glutamate is especially important in regulating the flow of substances in and out of neurons, which in turn plays a part in synaptic plasticity.

Many studies explore the precise role astrocytes play in learning and memory. In a study reported in 2013, scientists at the University of Rochester injected 300,000 immature human astrocytes into newborn mouse brains.[5] The human cells spread throughout the brain, grew into mature astrocytes, and replaced the mouse astrocytes. At the end of a year, each mouse's brain contained approximately 12 million human astrocytes.[6] The mice were much smarter than normal. They learned tasks faster and remembered what they learned longer.

While neurons in mice, humans, and other animals are identical, human astrocytes are larger than

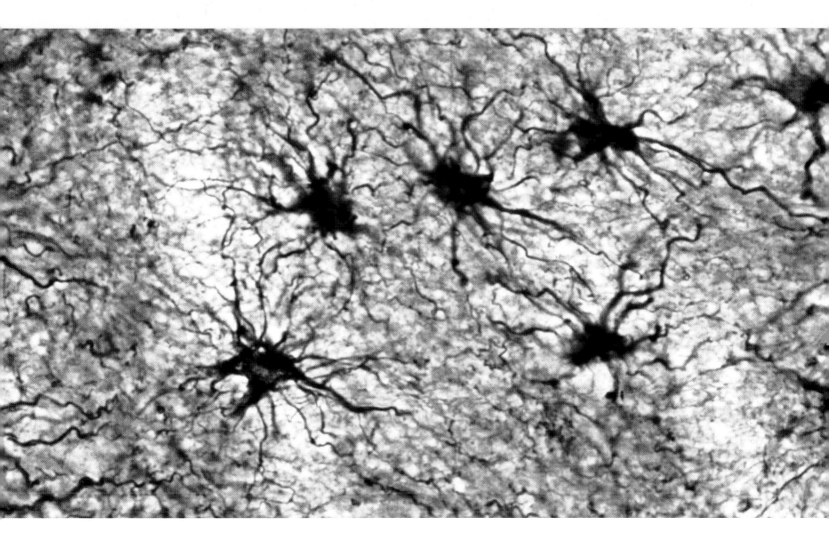

Astrocytes play an important role in reactions to nervous system injuries.

having greater intelligence than other animals because they have more dendrite-like cell extensions that control synapses. Besides influencing intelligence, astrocytes play a role in many brain diseases. While healthy astrocytes can strengthen synaptic connections, unhealthy or missing ones can cause Alzheimer's disease, Parkinson's disease, and brain cancer.

Microglia

Microglia are the brain's infection fighters. In healthy brains, microglia prune unused synapses and rewire neural connections. They also patrol the brain to look out for infections and injuries. Stanford University neuroscientist Katrin Andreasson calls microglia "the brain's beat cops."[10] When they find injured tissue, microglia release chemicals that help repair the tissue. In case of infection, microglia mobilize more immune cells to kill, ingest, and clear away damaged cells.

As with other glia, malfunctioning microglia can cause disease. For example, research led by Andreasson indicates improperly functioning microglia are largely responsible for the plaques, clusters of proteins between nerve cells, that lead to Alzheimer's disease. Andreasson's team also found that blocking EP2 receptors on microglia prevents or reverses Alzheimer's disease in mice. This is one of the most hopeful lines of research for the millions of human Alzheimer's sufferers. Microglia are also involved in other brain diseases. For example, scientists have discovered that when the human immunodeficiency virus (HIV) that causes acquired immune deficiency syndrome (AIDS) attacks the brain, it infects microglia and astrocytes. The wide array of research indicating the importance of glia in brain health and illness has opened new possibilities for understanding the brain and developing effective new treatments.

◢ Microglia and Alzheimer's Disease

Researchers at Stanford University demonstrated a chemical called PGE2 prevents microglia from dampening inflammation and sensing and destroying the plaques that cause Alzheimer's disease. PGE2 acts on EP2 receptors. As people and animals age, EP2 activity is more likely to inhibit microglia. This makes Alzheimer's more likely to develop, as ongoing inflammation injures synapses and neurons. The scientists genetically engineered mice that lacked EP2 receptors and found this restored the ability of microglia to sense and clear away plaques, thereby preventing Alzheimer's or reversing memory loss. Thus, drugs targeting EP2 receptors may be effective in preventing and treating the disease in humans.

SEVEN

THOUGHT-CONTROLLED MACHINES

A s scientists learn more about how the brain functions, they are exploring methods of undoing the devastating consequences of injuries and illnesses that leave people paralyzed or without limbs. Ultimately, researchers hope to repair or bypass nerve damage. However, until that goal is realized, neuroscientists, bioengineers, and computer scientists have made it possible for paralyzed people to control external machines with their thoughts. Similarly, thought-controlled mechanical limbs have improved life for people with amputations.

Thought-controlled limbs represent one of the most exciting areas of brain research.

BrainGate

A massive stroke in 1998 left Cathy Hutchison a quadriplegic, completely dependent on others and unable to speak but still mentally sharp. In 2012, doctors led by Brown University neurologist and bioengineer Leigh Hochberg implanted a computer chip called a BrainGate in the motor cortex of Hutchison's brain, within the area that controls arm motions. The chip, which is the size of a baby aspirin, has 96 thin electrodes that record neuron activity when Hutchison thinks about performing an action. The chip sends the thought signals to a computer, which translates them into commands to move a robotic arm. Hutchison learned to control the robotic arm by thinking about what she wanted it to do. She stared at a bottled drink on a table and imagined the robotic arm bringing it to her mouth. The arm did exactly that, and she drank from the bottle with a straw. Operating the robotic arm, called a brain-computer interface (BCI), represented the first time Hutchison performed an action on her own since her stroke.

Although this technology is not yet available to the public, scientists believe it will open a new world of independence for paralyzed people once it is perfected. BrainGate chips can control many machines, including televisions or kitchen appliances, and researchers hope paralyzed people will someday perform a variety of tasks just by thinking about them.

Brain-Computer Interfaces

Thanks to neuroscientists, surgeons, and computer, electrical, and biomedical engineers, the technologies that underlie BrainGate have come a long way since the idea of brain-computer interfaces was first explored in the 1970s. In 1973, electrical engineer Jacques Vidal of the University of California, Los Angeles, coined the term brain-computer interface and published one of the first studies on using brain signals to create a BCI. Then, researchers tested various brain chips on laboratory animals before neurologist Philip Kennedy of Emory University implanted the first BCI into a human in 1998. The device allowed a paralyzed man named Johnny Ray to control a computer cursor with his thoughts.

In 2001, John Donoghue of Brown University began developing BrainGate. Donoghue tested BrainGate in rhesus monkeys, and in 2002, he described how these animals controlled a computer cursor with their thoughts. In 2004, surgeon Gerhard Friehs implanted the first BrainGate chip into Matt Nagle, a man unable to use his arms or legs. BrainGate allowed Nagle to use his thoughts to control an

▲ Thought-Controlled Games

Thought-controlled machines are made for fun, as well as to help people with disabilities. Several companies now manufacture headsets with EEG sensors that translate peoples' brain waves into digital computer signals. The person can then use thoughts to control a movie or game. However, rather than tracking specific thoughts, the EEG sensors track the brain's state of concentration or relaxation.

Just by concentrating, headset wearers can control the action in games such as Mind Hunter. Headsets made by a company called MyndPlay allow people who view the company's movies to control the movie plot. Some doctors say these thought-controlled systems can help people improve their mental health by relaxing and focusing their thoughts. But most people who buy these products are simply intrigued by the idea of controlling a game or movie with their thoughts.

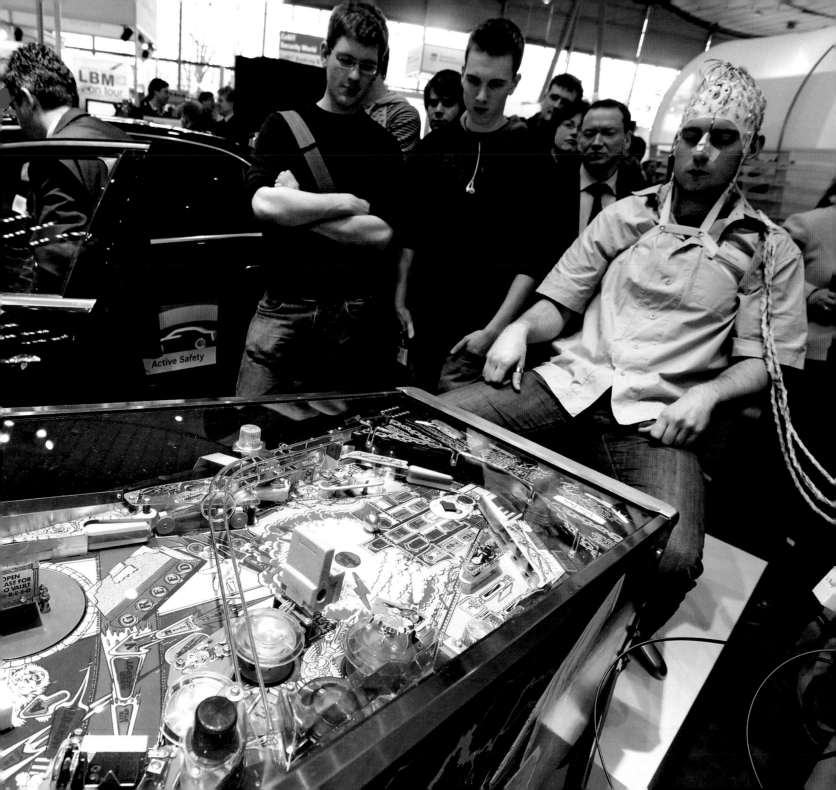

Experimental brain-computer interfaces have been used for many different applications, including playing a pinball machine.

artificial arm that moved a computer cursor, light switch, and television. Friehs called the results "spectacular, almost unbelievable. . . . Here we have a research participant who is capable of controlling his environment by thought alone—something we have only found in science fiction so far."[2]

Donoghue's team has improved BrainGate since his 2004 milestone, and other researchers are developing more types of BCIs that do not have to be implanted in the brain. Some of these experimental BCIs use electrodes placed on the surface of the scalp. Others use electrodes placed inside the skull but outside the brain itself. Scientists hope these noninvasive or partly invasive BCIs will prevent doctors from having to repeatedly go into the brain to change a chip's batteries when they run down. Some researchers are developing batteries that last for several years to reduce the need to keep replacing them.

The Bionic Leg

Bioengineers have made a great deal of progress with BCIs that control prosthetic limbs for people with amputations. In 2012, Zac Vawter, who lost one leg, climbed more than 2,100 stairs to the top of the Willis Tower in Chicago, Illinois. He used his mind to control the world's first thought-controlled bionic robotic leg. During the climb, Vawter's job was to think about climbing the stairs. The ten-pound (4.5 kg) aluminum bionic leg, with its two motors, sensors, belts, chains, and computer, did the rest.[3] University of Washington surgeon Douglas Smith redirected some of Vawter's severed nerves into the hamstring muscle on his right thigh. This technique, called targeted muscle reinnervation (TMR), was pioneered by Todd Kuiken of the Rehabilitation Institute of Chicago (RIC). Vawter's thoughts sent electric signals from his brain to his nerves. The computer translated the signals into movement commands carried out by the leg's moving parts.

▴ TMR to the Rescue

One of the biggest challenges in developing bionic thought-controlled prostheses was finding a method of hooking up a patient's thoughts with a prosthetic limb. Todd Kuiken's targeted muscle reinnervation method was key to making the limbs viable. Kuiken first used TMR in 2002 on a man named Jesse Sullivan, whose arms were both amputated after an accident. Kuiken rewired severed nerves that once controlled one of Sullivan's arms to muscles in his chest. Sullivan repeatedly thought about moving his arm, even though it no longer existed. The neural impulses kept the rewired nerves alive, and they established new connections with the chest muscles. As a result, Sullivan was able to control a bionic arm, allowing him to feed and dress himself, carry objects, and vacuum.

When Vawter's right leg was amputated in 2009 after a motorcycle accident, Smith determined he would be a good candidate to help RIC scientists led by Levi Hargrove test their new bionic leg. The US Army funded the research in an effort to find ways to help the many soldiers who lost limbs in recent wars. After Smith performed TMR, Vawter spent three years going back and forth to Chicago to help the researchers tweak the leg. Similar arm prostheses had been in use for several years, but perfecting the leg was more complicated, in part because a leg must bear a person's weight.

During the testing phase, the researchers asked Vawter to think about performing certain actions with his no-longer-present right leg to keep the rewired nerves alive. Nerves that receive no signals die off. The team used electrodes to record the signals Vawter's brain sent to the rewired nerves as he imagined a variety of actions, such as moving his ankle or raising his knee. Computer experts developed software that translated the neural impulses into commands for the bionic leg. The software also lets the computer learn from experience. It recognizes thought patterns and uses this information to predict what the next instruction to the leg is likely to be. This helps the leg operate smoothly.

Vawter's climb to the top of Willis Tower was an impressive demonstration of how far thought-controlled legs have progressed.

◢ Two-Way Communication

Bionic limbs allow people with amputations to perform actions they once thought were impossible, but users still cannot use the prosthetic limb to feel and sense objects. In 2014, several teams of researchers announced they successfully wired pressure sensors into the fingers of a bionic hand. The sensors send signals to a computer that transmits the signals into wires sticking out of a person's skin. This allows the person to feel the hardness, softness, or shape of the objects the prosthesis is touching. A Danish man named Dennis Sorensen, who lost his left hand in a fireworks explosion, helped test the sensors. Sorensen told *National Geographic*, "It's amazing to feel something that you haven't been able to feel for so many years."[5] Scientists hope to make the sensors work wirelessly so users will not need to have electrodes sticking out of their skin.

One weakness of normal prostheses legs is that they behave essentially as walking sticks that help with balance. Brain-controlled mechanical prostheses, however, can move independently to help the user climb stairs or slopes. The key to making a prosthesis act more like a natural leg was figuring out how to integrate the user's thoughts with the leg's mechanics. According to Vawter, "The bionic leg is a big improvement compared to my regular prosthetic leg. . . . This is a huge milestone for me and for all leg amputees."[4]

An $8 million grant from the US Army helped fund the development of Vawter's leg.

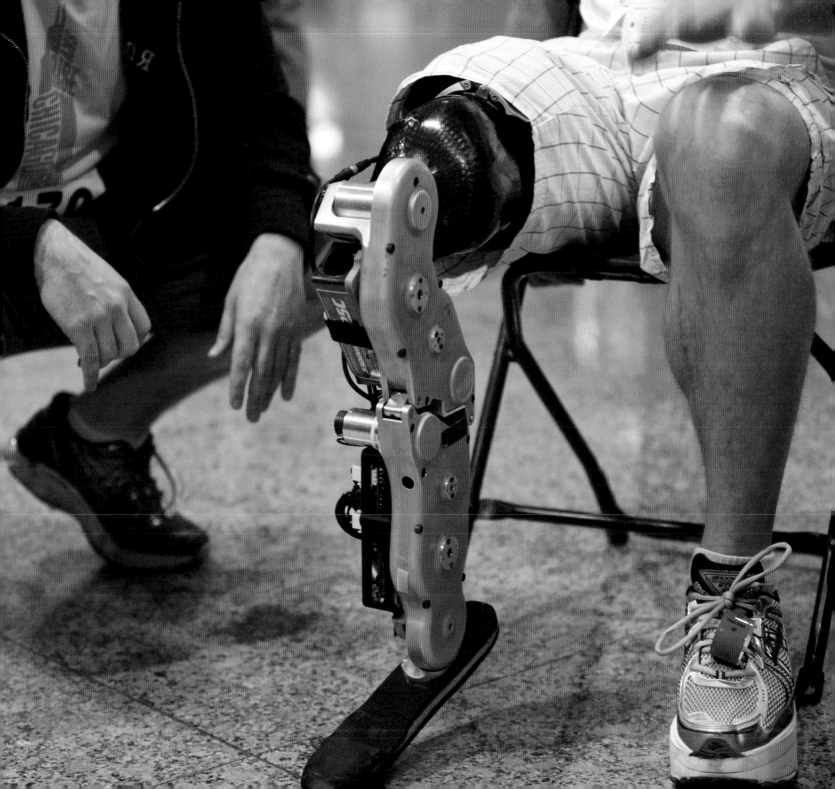

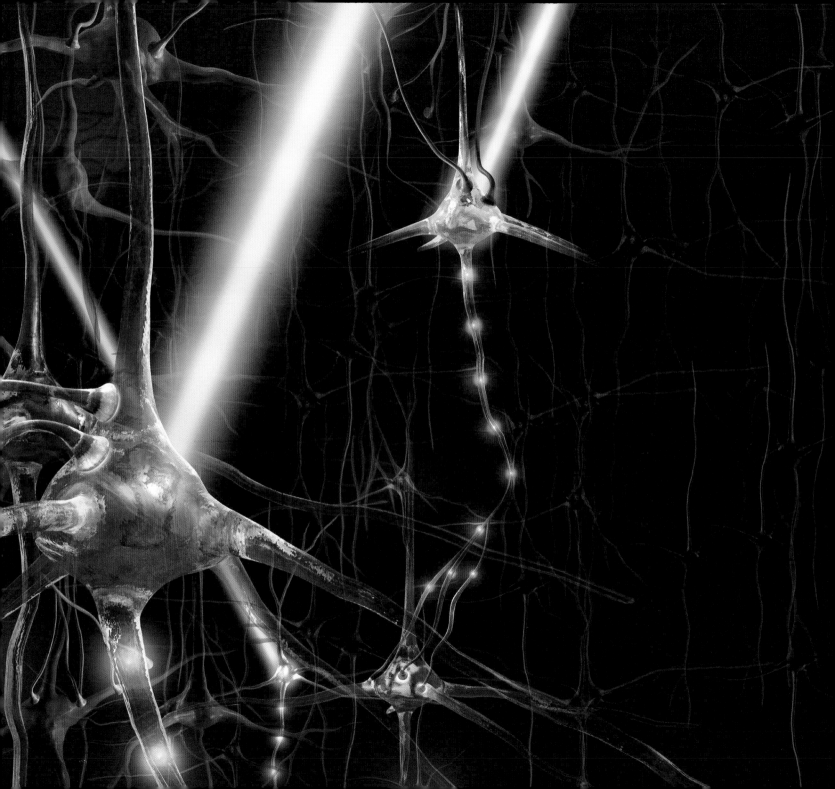

EIGHT

STORING AND DELETING MEMORIES

At one time, memories were an elusive concept that neuroscientists thought were likely encoded by neurons in the hippocampus. But recent research has shed light on how memories are encoded in specific cells and how they can be manipulated and erased. In a 2012 study, researchers Steve Ramirez and Xu Liu of the Massachusetts Institute of Technology (MIT) used optogenetics to prove memories are encoded in engrams in a region of the hippocampus called the dentate gyrus. They genetically engineered a mouse to have light-sensitive neurons in the dentate gyrus that would produce a protein called channelrhodopsin-2 when the neurons became active and involved in forming a memory.

Optogenetics technology enables researchers to alter memories within test animals' brains.

The researchers then placed the mouse into a box. It began exploring and received an electric shock to

Gene Therapy

Some scientists are using gene therapy—adding or deleting certain genes from DNA—to study memory and to develop methods of enhancing or erasing memories. For instance, Joseph Tsien of Princeton University discovered adding an extra NR2B gene, which controls neuron communication in the hippocampus, enhances a mouse's memory and its ability to perform complex tasks. Deleting NR2B impairs a mouse's ability to remember events or objects. In studies on other genes, Jerry Yin and Timothy Tully of Cold Spring Harbor Laboratory found adding an extra CREB activator gene to fruit fly DNA allowed the flies to learn a task ten times faster than normal. The CREB activator gene stimulates new connections between neurons. Conversely, fruit flies given an extra CREB repressor gene could not form lasting memories.

its feet. The researchers observed the neurons that were encoded with the memory of the shock and later stimulated those neurons with a laser. The mouse froze in fear as the memory was activated. The researchers found that once a memory is encoded, the same neurons that were active when it formed must be activated to retrieve the memory. The next step in the experiment proved the mouse's memory was encoded in an engram. The researchers euthanized the mouse and studied slices of its brain. They applied chemicals that react with channelrhodopsin-2 to the brain slices. Only the dentate gyrus cells in which the memory was encoded glowed green. This showed the neurons had been used to form memories.

Implanting a False Memory

Ramirez and Liu later figured out how to manipulate the dentate gyrus cells to implant a false memory in a mouse's brain, bringing notions from such science-fiction movies as *Total Recall* and *Inception* into reality. They put a genetically engineered mouse into a box. It spent 12 minutes exploring, but received no electric shock. The next day, they

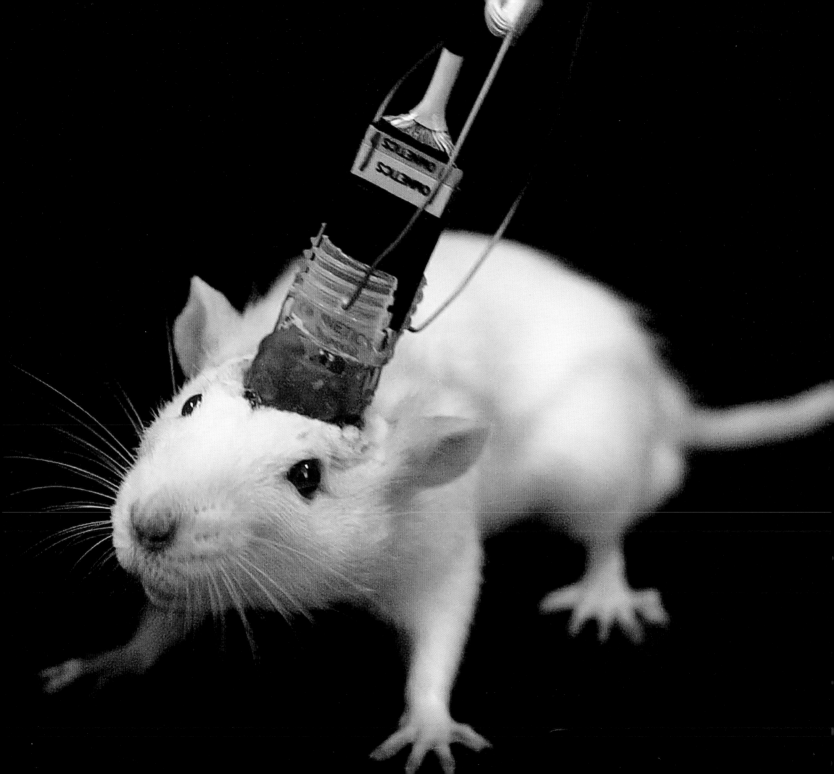

Artificial Brain Parts

Theodore Berger of the University of Southern California and Sam Deadwyler of Wake Forest University developed an artificial hippocampus, which they called a neural prosthesis. The researchers taught rats to press one of two levers to receive a food reward. As the memory of the task formed, the researchers used electrodes to record changes in the rats' brain activity between two areas of the hippocampus called CA3 and CA1. CA3 and CA1 interact to form long-term memories. The researchers then administered drugs that block interactions between CA3 and CA1 to disable the hippocampus. The rats no longer remembered the task.

Berger and Deadwyler used the brain activity recordings to create an electronic hippocampus in the form of a silicon chip. The chip duplicates the interactions between CA3 and CA1. The researchers hooked up the chip to the rats' brains and activated it. The rats remembered the task and chose the correct lever.

placed the mouse in a different box. They used a laser to activate the mouse's memory from the previous day. At that moment, the mouse received a shock to its feet. On the third day, the mouse was put into the first day's box. It froze in fear, even though it had not received a shock in that box. The researchers made sure the mouse could not have mixed up boxes one and two. The boxes smelled different and were made of different shapes and colors. The researchers also used control groups of mice. These mice received laser flashes that did not activate memories. This allowed the researchers to prove the laser flash did not cause the fear reaction in the experimental mouse.

Neuroscientists were amazed by the achievement of implanting a false memory into an animal's brain. "No one ever thought that you could actually, really do this," stated Sheena Josselyn of the Hospital for Sick Children in Toronto.[1] The research spurred new avenues of investigation in laboratories worldwide. According to a *Smithsonian Magazine* article, the MIT study "has launched a new era in memory research and could someday lead to new treatments for medical and psychiatric afflictions such as depression, post-traumatic stress disorder, and Alzheimer's disease."[2]

Theodore **Berger**

Theodore Berger is a professor of biomedical engineering at the University of Southern California. He spent more than 20 years developing an artificial hippocampus that can restore the ability to form long-term memories in people with severe memory loss. According to Berger, most neuroscientists think his ideas are unrealistic. But his success in using a primitive artificial hippocampus to restore a memory in rats is making other experts take him more seriously.

Berger has been performing acts people say are impossible for a long time. In 1976, as a Harvard University graduate student, he helped find the specific place in a rabbit's brain where memories form. The team recorded electric spikes in neurons and found patterns that recurred when a memory was forming in the hippocampus. In the 1990s, Berger began working on brain prostheses before other scientists considered the possibility they could be created.

Even though many questions remain unanswered, Berger and his team are testing his brain prosthesis in animals. He confesses he is a bit surprised by how far his "crazy" ideas have come: "I never thought I'd see this go into humans, and now our discussions are about when and how."[3]

The Chemistry of Memory

In other memory research, a study by neuroscientists André Fenton and Todd Sacktor of the State University of New York was named one of ten "Breakthroughs of the Year 2006" by *Science* magazine. The team showed that a molecule called protein kinase Mzeta (PKMzeta) is key to preserving long-term memories because it keeps the synapses involved in the memories active. Injecting a chemical called ZIP, which is a PKMzeta inhibitor, into the hippocampus of rats up to 30 days after the animals learned a task erased their memory. ZIP did not affect the rats' ability to relearn and form new memories of the original task or other tasks. Later research showed PKMzeta is involved in long-term memory storage in other brain areas as well.

For several years after this research, experts thought PKMzeta was the critical long-term memory molecule, especially after other scientists replicated the results in rats and various animals. In 2007, Sacktor went on to show PKMzeta must be continuously present in the cortex for stored memories to persist. In 2011, he found that adding extra PKMzeta to rats' brains enhanced long-term memories.

However, according to a *Nature* article, PKMzeta was "dethroned" as the magic memory molecule in 2013.

Two independent teams of researchers, one led by Richard Huganir of Johns Hopkins University and another led by Robert Messing at the University of California, San Francisco, wondered if ZIP, rather than PKMzeta, had caused the long-term memory results. Both teams deleted the gene that regulates PKMzeta in mouse embryos. Yet when the mice were born, all could form lasting memories of objects, places, and events. Huganir stated, "Our study pretty conclusively says that PKMzeta does not regulate memory. We were quite surprised."[4] His team was even more surprised to find that injecting ZIP into the mice that lacked PKMzeta erased established memories. This indicated ZIP acts on other molecules involved in long-term memory storage.

Sacktor responded to the 2013 findings by stating he believes a different gene may have compensated for the loss of PKMzeta, since this often happens when genes are deleted or nonfunctioning. Huganir disputed this claim because his research also showed deleting the PKMzeta gene in adult mice did not

◄ Memory Drugs

Scientists already know lifestyle changes, including diet and exercise, can improve memory. New research involves changing existing memories. Researchers are investigating drugs that can selectively block or delete traumatic memories. Memories with an emotional connection are stored and retrieved differently than other memories. Scientists believe these memories are connected with pathways in the amygdala, as well as in the hippocampus. In 2014, Edward Meloni of Harvard University reported the gas xenon, used in anesthesia, neutralizes the fear associated with a bad memory in rats. Xenon prevents neurons involved in recalling emotional memories from connecting with the amygdala.

Dutch researcher Merel Kindt found propranolol, commonly used to treat high blood pressure, can erase peoples' bad memories, suggesting it may be useful in treating PTSD and similar disorders. Giving people propranolol before asking them to recall a fearful memory erased the memory and prevented it from returning. Propranolol blocks the chemical adrenaline, which is essential for activating neurons involved in retrieving fearful memories.

impair memory. He suggested ZIP may target other proteins aside from PKMzeta and that any of these other proteins could also be important for long-term memory. Further research is needed to answer the questions raised by Huganir's findings.

NINE

REMARKABLE
POSSIBILITIES

Although scientists are making unprecedented progress in understanding the brain, neuroscientist R. Douglas Fields writes that the workings of this organ are still "the greatest enduring mystery of the human body."[1] There is still much work to do. Cutting-edge neuroscience research projects continue to build on new and emerging technologies and scientific breakthroughs, as neuroscientists worldwide make steady progress in their understanding of the brain. Some of the areas in which experts foresee dramatic medical and technical advances include brain-like computers, stem cells, gene therapy, and artificial brain parts.

President Barack Obama spoke in April 2013 about the cutting-edge research of the BRAIN Initiative.

Can Computers Mimic the Brain?

Numerous researchers are developing brain-like computers because they believe reverse-engineering the brain will reveal many of its secrets. Two of the best-known projects of this nature are SyNAPSE and SPAUN.

SyNAPSE, which is under development for the US government, simulates 530 billion neurons and 100 trillion synapses in a high-speed supercomputer to approximate the way the human brain operates.[2] SyNAPSE incorporates numerous advanced TrueNorth computer chips. One shortcoming of most computer chips is that they only allow one calculation at a time, whereas the brain makes many decisions and integrates many types of data at the same time. The postage stamp–sized TrueNorth chip contains thousands of individual processors that can perform 46 billion synaptic operations per second, allowing it to function similarly to a simple brain.[3] Including multiple TrueNorth chips in SyNAPSE gives it the ability to somewhat mimic the human brain.

The Semantic Pointer Architecture Unified Network (SPAUN) system, developed by Chris Eliasmith of the University of Waterloo, goes a step further than trying to simulate the brain's internal processing

A circuit board containing 16 SyNAPSE chips contains more than 250 virtual synapses per chip.

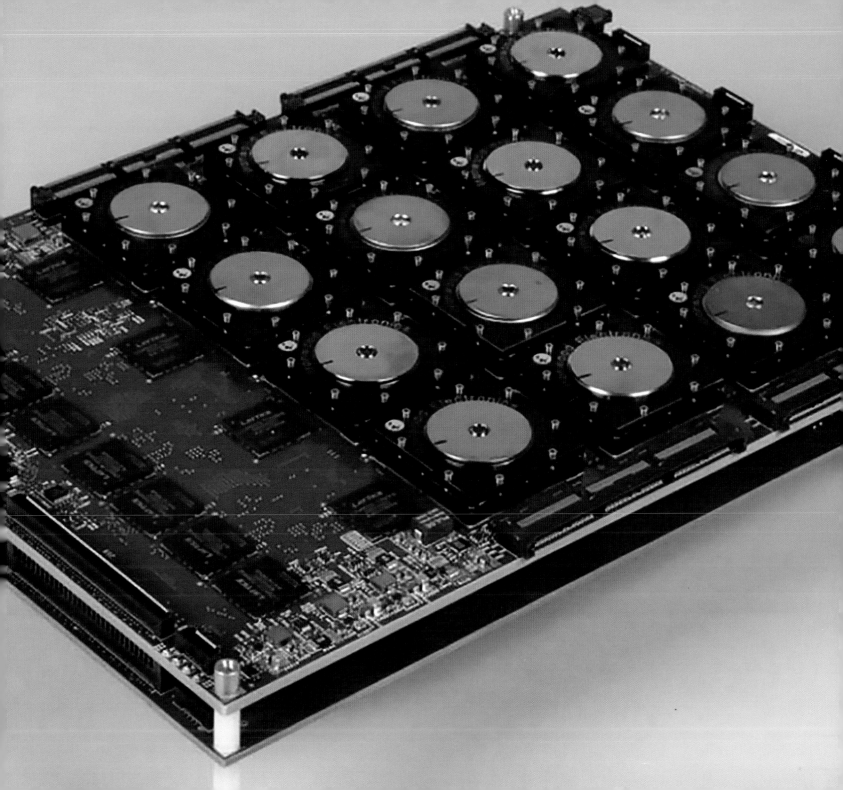

systems. SPAUN uses a digital eye to interpret images and simulate sensory input. A digital robotic arm then moves in response to neuron signals to simulate behaviors.

Even the world's most powerful supercomputers are unable to think the way a human brain can.

◄ Spare Brain Parts

It may someday be possible to replace damaged brain parts with prosthetic parts. Theodore Berger's artificial hippocampus is not the only brain prosthesis being tested. Researchers led by Matti Mintz at Tel Aviv University in Israel have created a synthetic cerebellum. The cerebellum is a portion of the brain that primarily coordinates movement. It interprets input from the cortex and brain stem and sends messages to areas of the brain stem that communicate with motor neurons. The brain stem transmits signals to and from the rest of the body and the brain.

Mintz's team built the synthetic cerebellum into a computer chip after analyzing recordings of signals to and from a rat's cerebellum. The team tested the chip, which sat outside an anesthetized rat's skull, after disabling the rat's cerebellum. The chip allowed the rat to learn a motor skill it should not have been able to learn with a disabled cerebellum.

The system also models the internal brain operations of more than 2 million neurons.[6] Each neuron is modeled after known types of neurons in various brain areas. These neurons interact with other neurons in the model in ways that are consistent with known facts about the neurotransmitters they use and the types of networked connections they make. For instance, neurons in SPAUN's basal ganglia are mostly GABA-producing neurons, just like those in the human brain. These neurons regulate data flow through the computer's cerebral cortex in a manner similar to the way real basal ganglia operate.

SPAUN can learn and remember new input, but unlike a real brain, SPAUN cannot learn completely new tasks. It also does not contain representations of all of the brain's structures—only the major ones. Researchers expect to improve SPAUN's capabilities as computer chips become able to perform faster calculations.

Regenerative Medicine

Besides understanding the brain, a major goal of neuroscience is to improve brain health. One of the fastest-growing areas of medicine, known as regenerative medicine, offers hope for people who suffer from brain diseases, as well as other types of disorders. Regenerative medicine involves replacing diseased or dead body cells with stem cells, which are immature cells that can develop into certain types of mature cells. Many stem cell studies that seek to replace nonfunctioning cells in brain diseases such as Parkinson's, Alzheimer's, and multiple sclerosis are underway.

In April 2015, researchers at Case Western University announced progress using a quicker alternative approach to stem cell therapy. This approach uses drugs to activate stem cells in the brain rather than growing the cells in a laboratory and transplanting them. The researchers found that two drugs approved for other purposes may be effective in treating MS in this manner. One drug, miconazole, is used to treat fungal infections. The other drug, clobetasol, treats inflammation. The researchers injected either miconazole or clobetasol into the brains of mice with MS. Both drugs activated oligodendrocyte stem cells in the brain, stimulating them to

Types of Stem Cells

There are three main types of stem cells. Embryonic stem cells come from embryos and are pluripotent, meaning they can develop into any type of body cell, depending on instructions they receive from genes and chemicals in their environment. Adult stem cells are found in many body organs. They are not pluripotent and can only develop into certain types of cells. Scientists reprogram adult stem cells to produce the third main stem cell type, induced pluripotent stem cells, which can develop into any type of body cell. Scientists are studying methods of using stem cells to treat or cure many diseases. Thus far, only adult stem cells are used routinely, usually in bone marrow transplants. Procedures using other stem cell types are still experimental. Scientists need to overcome the risks of embryonic or induced pluripotent cells multiplying uncontrollably and other technical issues before procedures involving these stem cells can be approved for medical use.

produce myelin. Mice paralyzed from MS were able to use their hind legs again. When the researchers applied either drug to human or mouse oligodendrocyte stem cells in a laboratory, the stem cells became myelin-producing cells. These results are promising, but it takes many years for cutting-edge research to lead to actual medical treatments. Experimental results must be replicated and proved to be valid by multiple researchers. Then, years of testing on animals and humans are required to ensure a treatment's safety and effectiveness.

Gene Therapy

The consequences of using experimental treatments on people before they are proved to be safe became evident in a case involving gene therapy in 1999. Gene therapy involves replacing defective disease-causing genes with normal genes. Doctors use tools called viral vectors to attach harmless viruses to a normal gene to get it inside body cells. The process is similar to the way viruses naturally infect living cells. During the 1990s, doctors believed gene therapy would cure many diseases. Even

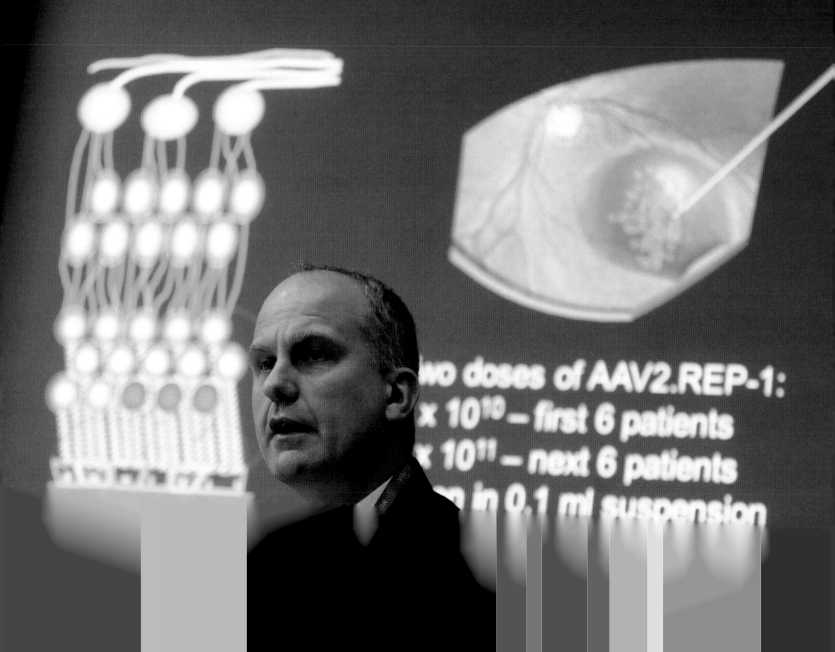

In January 2014, researchers announced the promising results of a gene therapy trial that used viral vectors to treat a rare cause of blindness.

though patients in experimental studies had adverse reactions when their immune systems attacked viral vectors, some doctors ignored the problems. In 1999, 18-year-old Jesse Gelsinger, who had a rare genetic liver disease, agreed to participate in a gene therapy experiment at the University of Pennsylvania. His immune system overreacted to the viral vector, and he died four days later. A subsequent investigation revealed Gelsinger's doctors had not disclosed the dangers to him. It also found federal regulatory agencies had not closely studied the safety of gene therapy. As a result, gene therapy trials were temporarily suspended. When they began again, they proceeded slowly, with added safety measures.

Many experts believe Parkinson's disease, which involves the progressive degeneration of dopamine-producing neurons in the brain, is a good candidate for gene therapy because doctors know it is caused by a dopamine deficiency. Standard therapy involves giving patients drugs the brain converts to dopamine, but this treatment tends to become less effective over time, and it does not help all patients. Thus, scientists are exploring ways of introducing genes that regulate dopamine production into appropriate brain areas. In 2014, a team of French researchers announced a newly developed combination of three genes involved in dopamine production effectively stimulated neurons to produce dopamine when injected into the brains of 15 people with advanced Parkinson's.[8] The combination is called ProSavin. Most of the patients experienced vastly reduced symptoms with few side effects. Further trials with more patients are planned.

The Future

With many ongoing projects exploring promising new treatments for brain illnesses and an explosion of investigations seeking to understand how the brain works, experts predict many new insights will continue to emerge in the coming decades. Given the complexity of the brain, disease cures will not

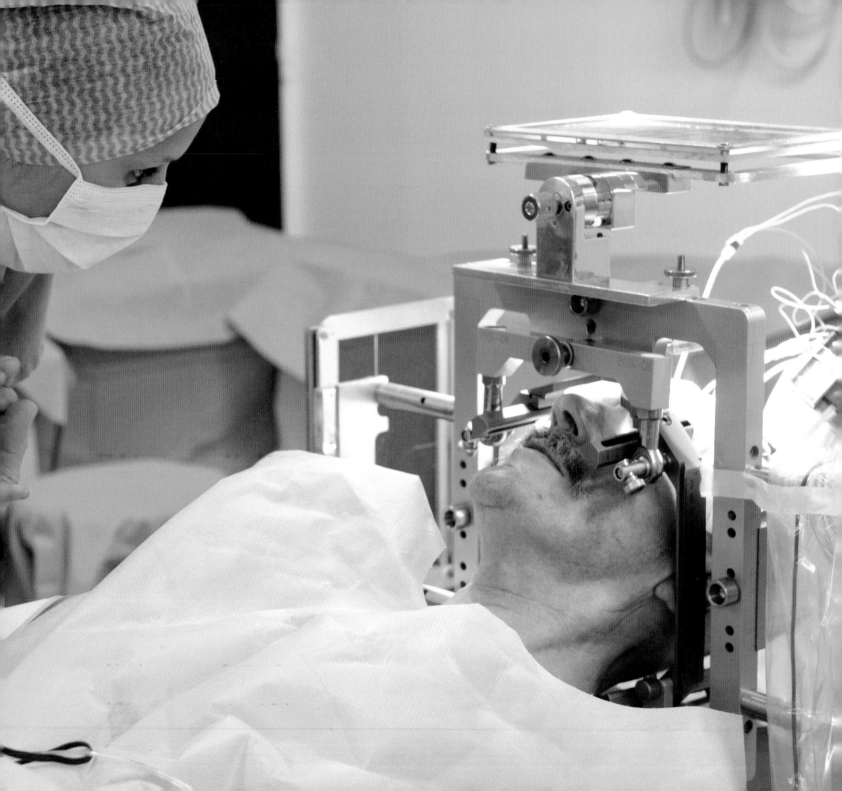

Parkinson's disease is a debilitating disease, but new, cutting-edge treatments and therapies may help slow or reverse it.

appear overnight. However, neuroscientists are optimistic steady progress will continue. As neuroscientists Gary Marcus and Jeremy Freeman wrote in their 2015 book *The Future of the Brain*, "There's never been a more exciting moment in neuroscience than now."[9]

ESSENTIAL FACTS

Key Discoveries

» **BOINC:** A technique called Barcoding of Individual Neuron Connections (BOINC) enables scientists to trace connections in the brain.

» **CLARITY:** The CLARITY technique makes it possible to view and highlight sections of transparent brains.

» **Filtering Information:** Researchers identified the brain circuit in mice that allows them to filter irrelevant information.

Key Players

» **Karl Deisseroth:** Karl Deisseroth of Stanford University led the team that developed the CLARITY technique.

» **Miguel Nicolelis:** Miguel Nicolelis of Duke University developed a brain-to-brain interface.

» **Rajesh Rao and Andrea Stocco:** Rajesh Rao and Andrea Stocco at the University of Washington demonstrated a human-to-human brain interface.

» **Steve Ramirez and Xu Liu:** Steve Ramirez and Xu Liu of MIT were able to implant false memories into mouse brains.

» **Theodore Berger:** Theodore Berger developed an artificial hippocampus.

Key Tools and Technologies

» **Brain Gate:** A computer chip called a BrainGate allowed patient Cathy Hutchison to control a robotic arm using her mind.

» **Electrodes:** Electrodes are used to record neuron activity.

» **Scanning Tools:** MRIs, fMRIs, EEGs, and PET scans allow scientists to view and study the brain.

Future Outlook

Future developments in brain science will build on the cutting-edge work being done today. Interfaces between brains may enable people to transmit thoughts and actions over long distances. Advanced computers will model the brain in more sophisticated and accurate ways. The improved understanding of the brain's structure and function will improve the outcomes of brain treatments and surgeries.

Quote

"The human brain, with its billion nerve cells, is the most complex piece of organized matter in the known universe."

—*Neuroscientist Christof Koch*

GLOSSARY

connectome

A wiring diagram of the connections between neurons.

dendrite

A short extension on a neuron that receives signals from other neurons.

engram

A biological trace in which neurons store memories.

gene

The part of a DNA molecule that transmits hereditary information and directs cell operations.

genome

An organism's complete set of DNA.

inflammation

Swelling.

interface

A point at which two independent systems or objects meet and interact.

mutation

A change in a gene.

neuroinformatics

The science of applying computer and mathematical models to organize and understand brain function.

neuron

A brain cell that sends electric signals.

neuroscience

The science that studies the nervous system.

neurotransmitter

A brain chemical that plays a role in communications between brain cells.

nucleotide

A chemical building block for DNA.

optogenetics

Technology that uses light to control genetically engineered neurons.

plasticity

The ability of connections between neurons to change.

prosthesis

An artificial limb.

receptor

A structure on neurons' dendrites that takes up neurochemicals.

stem cell

An immature cell that can develop into specific cell types.

synapse

A tiny gap between neurons over which chemical and electric signals are sent.

telepathy

Communicating with thoughts.

ADDITIONAL RESOURCES

Selected Bibliography

Kaku, Michio. *The Future of the Mind*. New York: Anchor, 2014. Print.

Marcus, Gary, and Jeremy Freeman, eds. *The Future of the Brain*. Princeton, NJ: Princeton UP, 2015. Print.

Trimper, John B., Paul Root Wolpe, and Karen S. Rommelfanger. "When 'I' Becomes 'We': Ethical Implications of Emerging Brain-to-Brain Interfacing Technologies." *Frontiers in Neuroengineering* 7 (2014). Print.

Further Readings

Carter, Rita. *The Human Brain Book*. New York: DK, 2014. Print.

Dwyer, Helen. *The Brain*. London, UK: Brown Bear, 2011. Print.

Websites

To learn more about Cutting-Edge Science and Technology, visit **booklinks.abdopublishing.com**. These links are routinely monitored and updated to provide the most current information available.

For More Information

For more information on this subject, contact or visit the following organizations:

Brain & Behavior Research Foundation

90 Park Avenue, 16th Floor
New York, NY 10016
646-681-4888
https://bbrfoundation.org

The Brain & Behavior Research Foundation awards research grants to neuroscientists and provides information about mental illnesses and neuroscience research.

National Institute of Mental Health (NIMH)

Science Writing, Press, & Dissemination Branch
6001 Executive Boulevard, Room 6200, MSC 9663
Bethesda, MD 20892
866-615-6464
http://www.nimh.nih.gov

The NIMH is a branch of the National Institutes of Health. It sponsors and conducts research on mental illnesses and brain function and provides public information about all aspects of the brain.

SOURCE NOTES

Chapter 1. Sending Thoughts from Brain to Brain

1. "Brain-to-Brain Interface Allows Transmission of Tactile and Motor Information between Rats." *Duke Medicine*. Duke University Health System, 28 Feb. 2013. Web. 21 July 2015.

2. Peter Saalfield. "Fusing Faculties of Mind." *Harvard Magazine*. Harvard Magazine, Mar.–Apr. 2014. Web. 21 July 2015.

3. Sebastian Anthony. "Harvard Creates Brain-to-Brain Interface, Allows Humans to Control Other Animals with Thoughts Alone." *Extreme Tech*. Extreme Tech, 31 July 2013. Web. 21 July 2015.

4. Doree Armstrong and Michelle Ma. "Researcher Controls Colleague's Motions in 1st Human Brain-to-Brain Interface." *UW Today*. University of Washington, 27 Aug. 2013. Web. 21 July 2015.

5. Ibid.

6. Gary Marcus and Jeremy Freeman, eds. *The Future of the Brain*. Princeton, NJ: Princeton UP, 2015. Print. 25.

7. Carl Zimmer. "The Brain: The Connections May Be the Key." *Discover*. Discover, 20 Mar. 2012. Web. 21 July 2015.

8. Gary Marcus and Jeremy Freeman, eds. *The Future of the Brain*. Princeton, NJ: Princeton UP, 2015. Print. 40.

Chapter 2. Mapping the Brain

1. Olaf Sporns, et al. "The Human Connectome: A Structural Description of the Human Brain." *PLOS Computational Biology*. PLOS Computational Biology, 30 Sept. 2005. Web. 26 Apr. 2015.

2. Michio Kaku. *The Future of the Mind*. New York: Doubleday, 2014. Print. 23.

3. Adam H. Marblestone, et al. "Rosetta Brains: A Strategy for Molecularly-Annotated Connectomics." *Anthony Zador Lab*. Anthony Zador, 2014. Web. 21 July 2015.

4. Ferris Jabr. "Sequencing the Connectome: Will DNA Bar Codes and a Sneaky Virus Change the Way Scientists Map the Brain?" *Scientific American*. Scientific American, 23 Oct. 2012. Web. 21 July 2015.

5. Anthony Zador, et al. "Sequencing the Connectome." *PLOS Biology*. PLOS Biology, 23 Oct. 2012. Web. 15 Apr. 2015.

6. Gary Marcus and Jeremy Freeman, eds. *The Future of the Brain*. Princeton, NJ: Princeton UP, 2015. Print. 95.

Chapter 3. A See-Through Brain

1. Andrew Myers. "Getting CLARITY: Hydrogel Process Creates Transparent Brain." *Stanford Medicine News Center*. Stanford University, 10 Apr. 2013. Web. 15 Apr. 2015.

2. Kerri Smith. "Neuroscience: Method Man." *Nature*. Nature, 29 May 2013. Web. 1 May 2015.

3. Michio Kaku. *The Future of the Mind*. New York: Doubleday, 2014. Print. 116.

4. Andrew Myers. "Getting CLARITY: Hydrogel Process Creates Transparent Brain." *Stanford Medicine News Center*. Stanford University, 10 Apr. 2013. Web. 15 Apr. 2015.

Chapter 4. Tracing Common Roots of Brain Disorders

1. "Psychiatric Genome-Wide Association Study Analysis Implicate Neuronal, Immune and Histone Pathways." *Nature Neuroscience*. PubMed, 2015. Web. 21 July 2015.

2. Ibid.

3. E. Fuller Torrey. *Surviving Schizophrenia*. New York: Harper Perennial, 2013. Print. 7.

4. Jaclyn Jansen. "Neuronal Circuits Filter Out Distractions in the Brain." *Cold Spring Harbor Laboratory News and Features*. Cold Spring Harbor Laboratory, 15 Dec. 2014. Web. 16 Apr. 2015.

Chapter 5. Body Defenses and Mental Illnesses

1. Elaine Setiawan et al. "Role of Translocator Protein Density, A Marker of Neuroinflammation, in the Brain during Major Depressive Episodes." *JAMA Psychiatry* 72.3 (Mar. 2015): 268, 271, 272. Print.

SOURCE NOTES CONTINUED

Chapter 6. The Forgotten Cells

1. R. Douglas Fields. "Neuroscience: Map the Other Brain." *Nature*. Nature, 4 Sept. 2013. Web. 21 July 2015.

2. Michael Balter. "Closer Look at Einstein's Brain." *Science*. AAAS, 17 Apr. 2009. Web. 21 July 2015.

3. R. Douglas Fields. "Neuroscience: Map the Other Brain." *Nature*. Nature, 4 Sept. 2013. Web. 21 July 2015.

4. Nancy Ann Oberheim, Steven A. Goldman, and Maiken Nedergaard. "Heterogeneity of Astrocytic Form and Function." *Methods in Molecular Biology*. HHS Public Access, Nov. 2012. Web. 21 July 2015.

5. Andy Coghlan. "The Smart Mouse with the Half-Human Brain." *New Scientist*. New Scientist, 1 Dec. 2014. Web. 21 July 2015.

6. Ibid.

7. Ibid.

8. Ibid.

9. Ibid.

10. Bruce Goldman. "Blocking Receptor in Brain's Immune Cells Counters Alzheimer's in Mice, Study Finds." *Stanford Medicine News Center*. Stanford University, 8 Dec. 2014. Web. 21 July 2015.

11. Jonah Lehrer. "Neuroscience: Small, Furry . . . and Smart." *Nature* 461 (15 Oct. 2009): 864. Print.

Chapter 7. Thought-Controlled Machines

1. Paul R. Wolpe. "Ethical and Social Challenges of Brain-Computer Interfaces." *AMA Journal of Ethics*. AMA Journal of Ethics, Feb. 2007. Web. 15 April 2015.

2. "Pilot Study of Mind-to-Movement Device Shows Early Promise. " *Brown University News Service*. Brown University, 8 Oct. 2004. Web. 21 July 2015.

3. Juan Perez Jr. "Mind Control Powers Prototype Bionic Leg." *Chicago Tribune*. Chicago Tribune, 25 Sept. 2013. Web. 21 July 2015.

4. "World's First Thought-Controlled Bionic Leg Unveiled By Rehabilitation Institute of Chicago." *Rehabilitation Institute of Chicago*. Rehabilitation Institute of Chicago, 25 Sept. 2013. Web. 16 Apr. 2015.

5. Josh Fischmann. "Revolution in Artificial Limbs Brings Feeling Back to Amputees." *National Geographic*. National Geographic, 22 Feb. 2014. Web. 16 Apr. 2015.

Chapter 8. Storing and Deleting Memories

1. David Noonan. "Meet the Two Scientists Who Implanted a False Memory into a Mouse," *Smithsonian Magazine*. Smithsonian, Nov. 2014. Web. 20 Apr. 2015.

2. Ibid.

3. Jon Cohen. "Memory Implants." *MIT Technology Review*. MIT, 23 Apr. 2013. Web. 6 May 2015.

4. Ed Yong. "Memory Molecule Dethroned." *Nature*. Nature, 2 Jan. 2013. Web. 20 Apr. 2015.

Chapter 9. Remarkable Possibilities

1. R. Douglas Fields. "Neuroscience: Map the Other Brain." *Nature*. Nature, 4 Sept. 2013. Web. 21 July 2015.

2. "IBM Simulates 530 Billion Neurons, 100 Trillion Synapses on Supercomputer." *Kurzweil News*. Kurzweil, 19 Nov. 2012. Web. 21 July 2015.

3. David Goldman, "IBM Builds a Brain out of Computer Chips." *CNN*. CNN, 7 Aug. 2014. Web. 6 May 2015.

4. Michio Kaku. *The Future of the Mind*. New York: Doubleday, 2014. Print. 134.

5. David Goldman, "IBM Builds a Brain out of Computer Chips." *CNN*. CNN, 7 Aug. 2014. Web. 6 May 2015.

6. Rebecca Boyle. "Meet SPAUN, the Most Complex Simulated Brain Ever." *Popular Science*. Popular Science, 29 Nov. 2012. Web. 21 July 2015.

7. Douglas Heaven. "Mini Human 'Brains' Grown in Lab for First Time." *New Scientist*. New Scientist, 28 Aug. 2013. Web. 16 Apr. 2015.

8. John Ericson. "New Drug ProSavin Offers Parkinson's Symptoms Relief in Phase 1 Trial." *Medical Daily*. Medical Daily, 9 Jan. 2014. Web. 21 Apr. 2015.

9. Gary Marcus and Jeremy Freeman, eds. *The Future of the Brain*. Princeton, NJ: Princeton UP, 2015. Print. xi.

INDEX

About the Author

Melissa Abramovitz is an award-winning author and freelance writer who has been writing professionally for 30 years. She specializes in writing nonfiction magazine articles and books for all age groups and has published hundreds of magazine articles, more than 40 educational books for children and teenagers, numerous poems and short stories, two children's picture books, and a book for writers. Abramovitz graduated from the University of California, San Diego, with a degree in psychology and is also a graduate of the Institute of Children's Literature.